I0413020

THE MILLENNIALS

Basil and Suzanne and Illusion

Roger K. Freeman

Copyright © 2015 Roger K. Freeman
All rights reserved.

ISBN: 1508633282
ISBN 13: 9781508633280

DEDICATION

To
Danielle May Trudel. Extreme Millennial woman!

Synopsis.

A MILLENNIAL TALE
Basil, Suzanne & Illusion

By Roger K. Freeman

When Millennial woman, Suzanne Guerrero, a part time waitress at Cape Cod's *East Sandwich Coffee Shop,* admired Basil Porter's shimmering Harley destiny prevailed. Their extended small talk became fiery and perilously co-terminal. As recent university grads they shared the grievance of the *Millennials' curse,* that unjust negative assessment of character assigned to those born between 1977 and 1994.

Their discovery of a shared interest to author a book dealing with the folly of war, societal ills of class, and to search for divine truth linked their interests that summer.

A stay at *The Bay-front Cottages* provides a perfect setting for writing until Kenneth Higgings, a retired master operative, befriends them and extends the offer of a paid journalistic venture deep in the cauldron of the Middle East. Their acceptance tears them from the accustomed comfort and safety of academia to interview and report on the plight of Syrian and Iraqi war refugees fleeing to Turkey.

This unexpected beginning immerses them in the ways of the world and the grimness of the dispossessed. Months later an unanticipated recall to stateside force Suzanne and Basil to a lifetime decision; to remain in journalism or seek other avenues.

Their choice reveals a mutual desire, to dedicate their lives to serving the needs of humanity. Having found their bliss, they forgive those detractors of the Millennials.

A MILLENNIAL TALE
Basil, Suzanne & *Illusion*

I'm Basil Porter. Please call me Basil and pronounce the 'Ba' as in *Ba Ba Black Sheep*. Thanks. First off, and as is often said; '*In the beginning*,' I was a happy kid and a bunch of my 'happiness' was my wonderful Hobby Horse. Mom gave me *Topaz* on my fifth birthday. I named him that very day. Topaz wasn't any ordinary horse-head on a stick. Oh no! He was as real and lifelike to me as the horses at our annual County Fair. Of course I knew he was all plastic and wood. He was elegant from his shiny brown coat, light yellow ears and a gorgeous soft flowing mane, blondish and befitting his name. He was my ticket to travel anywhere from my sunny room in our house to those faraway places of my imagination. I was secure in always knowing my fair and faithful companion would gallop at my command, carrying me handily on his soft leather saddle. I plunged my bare feet deep within his bright red stirrups as we rode off to anywhere. Imaginary? Yes!

When I was eight I still rode Topaz while waiting to say evening prayers with mom before bedtime. I had ceased my worldly travels. One Saturday morning after playing softball at the park I'd run home for lunch and found my Topaz gone. He hadn't ever left me. I found mom and said breathlessly that Topaz was missing.

She declared a truth that has affected my entire life. Mama spoke gently and held me close; "Basil, dear son, it comes a time we must let go, for Topaz to find a home with another child to love."

By the time I had nearly cried myself to sleep in her arms the anguish of Topaz' absence hit me. Then a thought struck me, one that told me that mama had suffered something like this when my dad died just before I was born. Mom had let go too.

I grew up a lot on that Saturday, alternately sobbing after my loss and fitfully churning in a half-sleep. Like mom had said, "It's like a pretend, Basil. Your Topaz was an illusion, a substitute toy for a real horse and he provided you pleasure for the time."

"He's never coming back, mama?" I couldn't tell from her reply if she was thinking of Dad or Topaz.

"No, Basil, he's never coming back."

I rarely look back, but in retrospect as I reached my immature fourteenth year my perspective hardened. Time had eased my pain. I knew the answer to my question on that Saturday. It was simple. My Topaz had been purchased that same day at mama's garage sale. My mom's decision was to remove my dependence on an outgrown fantasy. As it turned out her decision served me well.

I renamed my horse as a symbol of my independence. Forevermore his name is *Illusion*. He remained with me in my heart although it seems so very long ago. I had heard the word *Illusion* and as I approached manhood that word had gained much meaning to me. But yet, yes, I rode him as *Illusion* for years, now the symbolic Hobby Horse. I even found on the computer-lookup another definition that really zonked me; *[A topic to which one constantly reverts, a favorite topic given the slightest opportunity.]* Well, *Topaz, aka Illusion,* was more than a topic, but you see the parallels. Like so many of us, I had swallowed whole the illusions I was exposed to during my few years. My very being and lifestyle were predicated on what others thought appropriate. How to live, what to uphold, an existence in lockstep within a surround of nanny-like rules. Yes, I accepted those rules, thoughts, moralities, political jingoisms, and archaic religious teachings and writings both new and from the ages. One might ask how my early life differed from most of us and in retrospect it didn't. Even then and increasingly with time I recognized the power of repressive propriety and how extreme the power of authority is.

And then one day during an unreal symbolic gallop I turned rebel. Truly, I had enough. I pulled hard on *Illusion's* reins as my thoughts swung 180. My inner voice cried; *"Lift me from this mired morass and make me free!"* Well, that did it. My realization that *'If a man yields to conformity he forfeits his freedom.'*, that was the sting. I dismounted and figuratively walked my tired pony, *Illusion,* to a meadow by a cool stream and there I surrendered him. The thought racing through my head was indescribable. I had eradicated that multitude of controllers in my life or thought so. My autonomy was restored. I recovered my own self, my being, and I knew that my personal life at that moment was assured of freedom of choice, which rules to follow and those to disregard. That insidious little guilt monkey, the ones we endure riding on our backs, became belligerent, demanding; *'So, what now, rebel?'* and by that innate question had cleverly encouraged my return to the habitual action of bowing to self intimidation, coupled with self deception, followed by the desire to bow down in supplication.

But to that monkey my short answer is freedom with a full measure of reality. If you're behind the curve on this important matter, most assuredly you and I are among many. Now, at twenty years, I have a lock on it. I'm living with reality in fixed focus and there it shall remain. No more lockstep. And the monkey? He ran away with my rose colored glasses.

Yes, I have a new awareness. Yes, almost frightening it is. I thought, what if I'm going to be *'All about blank'* , a tabula rasa, as if my own mind is now absent of any prior experiences from birth, absent of conceptions. The genetically inherited axioms exist and further complicates the matter of a genuine functioning reality. Starting from scratch-Not! Obviously I must use my 'gathered information' to accomplish the intent of an age old euphemism; *Separating the wheat from the chaff.* But no, my conscious awareness asks a question; How? Chaff is overabundant among the wheat and I add it applies well to everything; politico, religious, cultural, social, ethics- ad infinitum. At first puff it appears that I must study every facet of life and after placing all of it in appropriate piles of true or false then determine my reality. Impossible you say? Right on!

A logical approach is called for. My essential freedom is the main ingredient for the task. Discharging the chaff on sight is elementary. What remains is the decision; to wit: which of these multitudinous subjects gets first billing? Yes, it's almost time to exercise that new freedom. Horace's imperative to have the courage to think for yourself hung on in my mind.

But then, my thoughts rang to what to do about those pesky things called human traits or characteristics and what those words really mean? I tried a list: anger, avarice, faith, belief, malice, revenge, guilt, intent, passion, love, lust, understanding, jealousy, prejudice, pride, awareness, duty, obligation, empathy, intelligence, comprehension, suffering, consciousness, free will, mindfulness, imagination, reason, willed action, that tribal coming together called culture, and instinct; an impulse more natural than reasoned. Instinct raised a red flag. I recalled that instinct is within us from birth and perhaps different than the animals in that we may reject or accept our instinctual inputs, as we are afforded the freedom of the explicit or implicitly allowing instinct to have its way.

And in my thought I questioned the presence of the robot, that imprimatur of the mind. Who? Is that me? Oh my, yes. The He - She - It of meaningful and automated direction. My robot directs me so much that my mind on some days takes a leave of absence from the drudgery of repeated chores, even driving, a sabbatical to provide time to think of the likeliest thing, whatever that is.

⇥ ⇤

After my final year at the University I fulfilled my dream of a long awaited vacation. I've wanted to visit Cape Cod for ages. This was the year. My enthusiasm hit fifth gear as I crossed the Cape Cod Canal at the Sagamore Bridge on my Harley. You ask? Yes, my Harley is part of my current rebellion.

At the roundabout, called a rotary in New England, I chose the slower road, *Highway 6A,* called the *Route of the Craftsman,* a friendly and less traveled road worming its way along the Cape's north shore. I'd driven the highway from Boston. My appetite signaled. I slowed at a neat little place with a bright red sign over the entrance: *East Sandwich Coffee Shop.* Negotiating the gravelly entrance to park I entered and found it to be the essence of friendly, simple and quaint. As I slipped onto a counter seat a bouquet of fresh coffee mesmerized me. Then a cute and snappy waitress handed me a menu, asking;

"May I help you, sir?"

"Yes, of course. Coffee and give me a minute with the menu."

She returned with my coffee. I asked, "How about the shrimp platter with fries?"

"I'll check on that. Be right back," Returning from the kitchen smiling, she said, "Yes. They do."

"That's fine. May I ask, why didn't you say; 'We do?'"

She leaned toward me as if to share a confidence, arching her back kittenishly. I caught myself looking.

"You're the first customer who asked that. I'm occasional help during the noon rush. Tourist season has begun and I'm still thinking in terms of them and me."

"I shouldn't have asked."

She smiled. "It's Okay. I'm Suzanne Guerrero."

7

"Nice to meet you, Suzanne. I'm Basil Porter," I offered my hand gently.

"Your white Harley out there?"

"Yes, it is. You guessed right and I'm another tourist on vacation."

"Somehow I thought so. Your bike is really classy."

"I guess one could say it's in a class of its own. Tell me, Suzanne, do you assume that people who ride motorcycles are in a discrete class?"

Suzanne answered haltingly, "Gosh, I never thought of it like that, but any such assumption implies identical status to the riders, while their common attribute may be limited to their mode of transportation. Why did you ask?"

"I shouldn't have. Just a freakish throwback from my interest about class and societal values. Can you spare a couple of minutes to talk?"

"Until the next customer appears, Basil. Take a table. I'll bring your lunch," Suzanne replied, while suppressing a growing apprehension.

"Yeah, okay, I'll sit at that table over there," I said, wondering why, without any predisposition to mention class I'd plunged ahead so pointedly.

A minute later Suzanne served lunch, saying, "Here you are." She sat opposite me, "Are you a student, Basil?"

"No. Just finished up. Oh, I get it. You picked up on my viewpoint on class. It was rude of me to be so abrupt and ask such silliness. Been out in the sun too long I guess."

Their eyes met at his self-effacement.

"I understand. I just graduated myself and my head is still up there someplace."

"Am I right to ask, you are one of us, another *millennial*, Suzanne?"

"Oh yes, and I suppose I'm topped off with all those negative characteristics used to define us. You are too!"

"I fill the definition. Time-wise I'm a cultural upstart, unemployed and happen to be from Boston, you know, Fenway Park - Red Sox nation!"

"Those are fine qualifications. I'm a Chicagoan. This is my first venture from the windy city."

"I'm glad you're here, Suzanne. Why Cape Cod?"

"I've always been fascinated by this giant sand spit and heard such nice things."

"Is it like you thought? Are you having a good time?"

"Oh, yes. It's paradisiacal to me. I came to absorb this place and I hope to develop my writing skills."

"Tell me, please, what did you study?"

"Philosophy and Religion. How about you?"

"Political science and mathematics. My real love is math."

"I heard a joke, its author unknown; the definition of a Millennium."

"I'm all ears."

"A Millennium is something like a Centennial only it has more legs," Suzanne recited. Their laughter caught onto all within earshot. She went on, "Our subject specialties aren't particularly millennial are they?"

"Not at all. Our accusers have it wrong, insisting we're driven by avarice and lust for the big bucks and the world's luxuries!"

"But mathematics, Basil! Never would have guessed that one. My take on mathematics is its free and independent status like it floats around without contingencies. You know, I suspect philosophy may be somehow related."

"You know Suzanne, I guessed from the beginning you didn't sound like a waitress."

"That gets us back to the *class* word. Gosh Basil, I'm surprised you're so judgmental. Yes, I'm here and proud to be waitress class."

Basil's red flag went up, "You're right; I ran directly into a human complexity didn't I?"

"Kind of. I never thought riding a classy motorcycle called for an analysis of our societal faults or prejudices. But you know, in a way we all play the class game. I suggest you avoid hoisting Mr. Basil up by his own petard!"

"I'm sorry. I really uphold equality," Basil reddened, choking on his fries.

"Why not start this dance on the other foot? I waitress to earn a few dollars."

"My apologies for stomping on your feet. I haven't danced well, have I?"

"Let's loosen up, Basil. Tell me a bit about yourself and your obsession with class."

"This problem of class has been gnawing at me since I became aware of its influence in society. Class permeates our entire world in a multitude of ways, Suzanne. It feeds the areas of hate and prejudice very handily. Class supports a dearly held status quo. Those judgments once made place barriers to fulfilling the admonition to '*love thy neighbor.*'"

"I'll say this, Basil, from both my studies of philosophy and religion I can tell you that searching for a classless society is futile, like searching for nirvana. It draws you to the sleep of reason."

"I'd like to talk to you more, Suzanne."

"You're socially aware Basil. I'd like to talk more too, but here come some customers. Gotta go. There's a lot of nice places to stay around here. Check out the ad rack over there."

"Thanks, Suzanne. Will do. See ya."

Basil Porter left with a brochure and a warm thought; '*Suzanne is a really sweet gal.*'

Biking '*Down-Cape*' along Route 6A, he spotted a sign: '*Cottage Rentals.*' It was at East Road, a left turn towards Cape Cod Bay. The brochure read: *Bayfront Seasonal Rentals. One and two bedroom cottages on the beach at Cape Cod Bay.* It had a nice ring to it. He left his Harley on the pavement at East Road and walked on the sand to a long row of brightly painted cottages. A woman in jeans and work clothes was repairing a screen on the door of the third cottage. She heard the scrunch of his biker boots and turned facing Basil in the afternoon sun.

"I hope I didn't startle you, mam. How much are the cottage rentals?"

"Give me a hand putting this door on its hinges and I'll tell you," she replied, struggling with the door.

He held the screen door as she slipped the hinge pins in place.

"I'm Kay Higgings. This is a one bedroom unit here. My husband and I lease on a monthly or seasonal basis. Some folks stay from Memorial Day through Labor Day."

"Hi Kay. I'm Basil Porter. Nice beach, How is the swimming?"

"The beach is public, but it's rare to see what one would call crowded. I'll tell you now, Cape Cod Bay water has a distinct coolness. We're on the north side. If you want warmer water beaches you should go look on the south side."

"I'm used to cool water, Kay. Fishing pretty good?"

"Most the time. Every cottage has fishing gear and you must have just driven by the bait store. Where are you from, Basil?"

"Northshore. Just up the pike from Boston."

"Well, welcome to the Cape. I'm sure you'll like it. Something I want to tell you though. It's the sand. This is a sandy place, especially when the wind comes up. We get a lot of bikers, so my hubby built a nice tight shed for the bikes," Kay pointed to a big shed with overhead doors.

"Good idea. I'd like to see one of the cottages."

"Of course, Mr. Porter. One or two bedrooms?"

"Kay, please call me Basil. One bedroom."

Kay opened the *#3* cottage and continued with her chores. The cottage was neat. Modern kitchen, microwave, fans, clean. The knotty pine walls diffused a soft glow, a light pumpkin hue so reminiscent of fifty years ago. Basil stepped back outside.

"What do you think, Basil?" Kay shouted against the breeze.

"If the price is right I'll rent it until the end of the month and then make a decision about longer."

"I can do that. Let's go inside and write it up."

Basil got settled in and that was pretty much the end of his first day on Cape Cod. He returned to route 6A and picked up some grub at the East Sandwich market and taking Kay's advice rolled the Harley into the shed.

My night was one of reading and then hitting the sack. My thought before sleep turned to writing, an ambition that had lurked in my mind for a long time. Mostly I wanted to write of the wisdom of the great contributors to mankind, more particularly to search out what guidance they could offer today's world, knowing full well that I might settle on something else.

⊷⊶

The morning came too soon. I snapped awake, startled by the thought I'd never left home. Congeries of seagulls screamed an unrelenting cacophony near my window. My *G-Shock Casio* said 6:10. Sliding across the bed to look out I did a double-take. There stood Suzanne Guerrero, the waitress, tossing chunks of bread in the air. In my native Gloucester these ubiquitous birds gather at the sight of food, so O.K., but why is *she* here? The instance of Suzanne's presence next to my cottage wasn't clarified until mid-morning.

I found some tired fish bait in my freezer and put it to work. Fishing off the beach was easy. I set some poles in the sand and waded in the light surf. The tide was up and the sun was hot. Not much success, but enough to touch off the charcoal grille on the deck.

A *Jeep* approached. Suzanne drove. Her surprise showed as she braked where I stood.

"What are you doing? Aren't you Basil?"

"I could ask the same of you. Your seagulls are good alarm clocks. You are Suzanne."

"You know very well I am. Are you staying here and what is that you're doing?"

"Yes, and I'm cleaning fish. C'mon for lunch if you like."

"I'll bring stuff. Be there in a few," she said slipping into cottage four.

Basil paused for thought; *'I've only just got my degree and on the second day of vacation this notably attractive woman is suddenly coming for lunch. Am I dismayed? Of course not! But my raison d'etre is to work - to do some serious mental gymnastics. What to do? Down boy! Don't let life get upended by this first girl you meet.'* I knew my self advisory went nowhere.

"Hi Basil. I brought this and some chips," she handed me a bucket of potato salad.

"Thanks Suzanne. Tell me, are you staying next to my cottage?"

"Yes. How shrewd of you to notice," she replied with a giggle.

"That was you this morning feeding the seagulls."

"I've been doing that every morning. I think they stand around waiting until the sun comes up. Did we wake you?"

"Well, yeah, kind of, but that's Okay. Being my first day here I should be up early."

Suzanne shoveled potato salad on my plate and refilled my coffee mug, saying, "I must ask, Basil. Did you pick this place to settle this summer?"

'I'd better tell her,' I thought, *'if only to explain the real reason I'm sitting here having lunch.'*

"I'm here to get my thoughts together, I'd like to try my talent at writing. Maybe try a book, stuff I think important. My biker-bag is loaded with books."

"Are you serious? You're kidding! You came on vacation to hit the books, c'mon, really? This is sheer coincidence. I guess we're on the same tack."

"I'm serious. This is exactly why I'm here, I want to re-think some stuff and have some fun."

'I was *rattled by what I thought she had said'* "Do you sail in Chicago?"

"Oh yes, we have lots of water. I love it. I don't know if you're ready for this, Basil. We may both be certifiably crackers. I must tell you, I came here to drive my Jeep on the dune trails. I've always wanted to come here, besides, I plan to write on the beach. I hope it takes all summer."

'I felt a pulsating in my head; my perception cantilevered on a cliff, attempting to balance the thought that Suzanne is beginning to sound like some kind of intellectual.'

He mumbled, "Don't wake me, Suzanne. Let me bask in this illusory paradise."

"Let's talk about what we've learned," Suzanne said, "I remember something about math from way back, Basil. Wasn't a Greek named Pythagoras into math?"

"Yes, as I recall, I think you're right, and may I assume you're on nodding acquaintance with Socrates?"

That broke the ice. Our laughter climaxed in crescendo.

She spoke, "You're serious aren't you? You know Basil, he said; *'Gnothi seauton,'* *Know Thyself.* I can tell you this; philosophy begins when we learn to doubt those things we're taught to hold high like senseless dogmatism and axiom driven crap."

Basil interjected, "How brave you are! I've one for you; *'To thine own self be true.'* That was *Polonius in Hamlet.*"

"And then, Basil; Polonius said, *'Then canst not then be false to any man.'*"

"You are real aren't you, Suzanne? This is the real you isn't it?"

"You mean like do I subscribe to these words?"

"Exactly what I mean."

"The truth, Basil, affirmative. I do."

"I believe you. I want to tell you the reason I'm here. Somewhere back there I hit a wall. I've been in a quandary, choking on a thicket of questionable facts and beliefs and a slew of establishment stuff. I've drowned in stylized recycling of familiar rhetorical themes and socially acceptable clichés. I've lived it, Suzanne, and I've dumped a bunch of it. Now I'm in the formative stages of finding my own way; you know, like that inevitable path to the mountain peak."

"You talk like you've found your path. Like Dr. Paul Tillich wrote; You've found '*The Courage To Be.*' Looks to me like a light went on. I've had some of the same thoughts. Instead of drowning on rhetoric, Basil, how about a swim before the tide gets so far out we can't reach it?"

We washed the dishes and later we raced down the beach. Suzanne splashed me with her icily cupped hands filled from the nippy receding wash. We were nearly waist deep when I stopped for breath.

"So tell me. How much of the world are you changing?" she asked, splashing me gently.

"I'll answer that, smarty. I'll borrow a Kafka-esque aphorism. He wrote, '*A cage went in a search for a bird.*' You get that? I'll tell you. His phrase applies so well to political tyrants searching for a very large cage in which to place their citizenry. Freedom in the cages, not! Now that's a change I'd like to make."

"You've made a case, Basil. Obviously you will change the political spectrum of the world this summer," Suzanne teased with her incredulous smile.

"Perhaps I've slightly over-stated, Suzanne. Let me ask you; I've never been to the sand dunes. Could we drive to the dunes someday?"

"I'm working at the Coffee Shop tomorrow and Thursday. We need a full day to hit the trails, but if you like, we could visit some nearby dunes. How about Friday?"

"That's great. I can fish for a couple of days and we can talk about writing and go swimming too."

⟞⟝ ⟞⟝

We ate breakfast at the Coffee Shop on Friday. Later we observed the de rigueur of so many tourists searching the attractive shops dotting the highway. Suzanne parked the Jeep near an entrance to the dunes in the Town of Barnstable. We were surrounded by a sea of tall grass among the board-walks. Stepping closely and gingerly around the green clusters we skipped over the random algae-green tidal inlets. While tiptoeing near the dunes' coarse sandy elements, Suzanne spoke of how sharply they contrasted with the surf's greenish diamonded scintilla.

"Walking in deep sand wasn't meant for everyone, Suzanne. I will say this vista more than compensates," Basil raised his voice against the breeze and the screaming gulls.

"It's probably good for us. I've read that Aristotle said that walking provides a philosophical outlook. If you want, we could stop and do something really nice."

"C'mon, Suzanne, I'm certain you didn't bring me here for that did you?"

"Oh, for crap's sake! Of course not. I meant we could talk about the nice things in life, like how to perceive their beauty."

Basil said weakly, "Of course. My misunderstanding. Gee, Suzanne, you know so much about me. I know you just graduated from the university and even why you came to the Cape, but otherwise I know so little. How about it? Want to share some stories?"

"I knew this had to happen. You know what, Basil? I'm glad we're free agents so we can walk away from our brief subtle innocence. I want you to know I haven't deliberately deceived you. I think our mutual interests captured us, at least it did me. Now is the time. I'm compelled to face the truth and tell you of my past."

"You make your past sound downright sinister. Look, I don't really have to know; we can always work together on a book. Why not remain as we are, free of complications and without attachments," Basil replied weakly, casting an empty look.."

"Oh, Basil, this can't work! I don't know what to say. If you'd rather, why don't we end everything. You can get on your Harley and disappear forever."

"No. No! I don't want. I'm a big boy now and I sense you share with me that we have something more. Somehow there's something existential about us. If we avoid the issues it may be to our sorrow. I'm long on committal, sweetheart."

"Come here and hold me, Basil, because I'm going to cry. I'll tell you all about my life, every dark corner of it, and if you leave me, well, I'm sorry. God knows I need you."

"Just let's talk like it isn't us, like this is some storybook thing. My mother once said; 'like a pretend.' I promise I'll make no judgments."

"Okay, Okay. Well, first, I was born out of wedlock, illegitimate as they say. I never knew my father. My mother tried to keep me, but when I was about four my aunt took over. Ma was desperate for money and needed to work. She had no job skills but after a while she got regular work at a fast-food place near where we lived on the south side."

"I think you're about to tell me you were a street child"

"More than you know. I was street-smart at a young age. When I was ten I got caught up in peddling drugs - anything the traffic needed. I was a courier of sorts and small time local mule. It was easy because I could run fast and I learned to hold my tongue everywhere - know what? I didn't steal."

"Did the law get to you?"

"Never. I had to stop. Someone shot my boss. I was lucky; I got out of it when I was thirteen. After that I stayed home a lot except I did go to school. I remember how my aunt walked me to school and walked me home a lot."

"Such a life, Suzanne!"

"You ain't heard it all yet, brother!"

"Oh, look. Let's stop. You're out of that life. Why can't we call that enough?"

"I'm bent on full disclosure, Basil. I guarantee this will test your will severely."

"Aw shit, Suzanne, I don't want to hear it!"

"You mean you've heard enough! You're figuratively warming up your motorcycle right now aren't you Basil?"

"No! God help me, no. Suzanne, embrace me please, sweet one!"

"Okay, I am. But, like the hawker said: *But wait! There's more..*"

"Go ahead then. Your story is killin me."

"This isn't pleasant, Basil. I met a boy. Our blood ran hot. I was fifteen. Yes, we did all that. We were in love or whatever euphemism defines lust. My aunt dragged me to the doctor. He said I was pregnant. We met the demands of family and married. He left school and got a construction job. We lived at my aunt's place."

"You were a mother at a young age," Basil said flatly.

"No. There was no pregnancy. No baby, and then no husband."

"What happened?"

"He was killed in a horrible construction accident. I kept his name. That's why I'm Suzanne Guerrero."

"I'm sorry. What else can I say?"

"I've tried to get my life straightened out, so far I've been okay. You know, Basil, youth is a trying time."

"You've been stretched to the limit. It's almost unbelievable, what you've endured. You still went to the university and graduated. I congratulate you for that."

"I must tell you how I happened to go to the university. My husband's insurance paid for it. We were happy together even though we had no child. He was a dear man. His insurance took me through it."

"This is a poor time to speak of it, Suzanne, but I'm compelled to tell you that your past hasn't influenced me to leave you. It's not pity. We will transcend it. I mean it, so please, let's not lose our lives to the past."

"I need to rest, Basil. Come with me, hold me and talk to me. By the way, tell me something of yourself. After that delusional pony, what did you do?"

"Not very exciting, honestly. I cut a lot of grass and when I was old enough I worked at the docks doing any job. I worked the fishing boats whenever I could. I helped my mother keep the place up. She took in roomers when I entered the university, so my bedroom became a cubby-hole next to the old pantry. I had a scholarship for a year and I'd saved enough working on the fishing boats to pay my way."

"Sounds like you were such a good boy."

"Not exactly. I'd lost my get-out-of-jail-free-card, so I spent a few nights in the local pokey because of what I call civil disobedience. No felony charges, fortunately."

"You're surely candid with your confessions, young man."

"Pleased to confess. I didn't arrive in town on a white horse, nor a suit of armor."

"You're not Sir Galahad, but you thrilled me."

"I peeked down your blouse."

"I know you did. We girls notice."

"Oh yeah."

"What better way to spend a glorious afternoon, Basil, than here at the dunes?"

"You seem to have a sort of obsession about the dunes, Suzanne. Like you said, it's one reason you're here. What makes them special for you?"

"I'm so obvious. Yes, I'll tell you. I find a presence here, like I've transcended the hustle of life, a sort of sanctuary."

"You're not talking escape. You find peace and solace here. The dunes seem to be part of your being." "I "I desperately need to tell someone."

"You needn't bare your soul to me."

"Actually Basil, before I finish you may decide you're talking to a looney."

"I plead then you let it all out. I'll not sit in judgment. Liking the dunes doesn't qualify for some strange psychiatric disorder. Please don't belittle yourself."

"That's fair. So I guess I may as well let it all out. First, Basil, my attachment to the dunes is their isolation, the irresistible silence, and for whatever reason I'm curious what forbidding secrets they may hold. These dunes have a depth and I sometimes sense a sort of hostility."

"I'm listening, Suzanne. There's an odd meaning in what you've said."

"Yes, and even more, I find an essential interaction about them. This should confirm my craziness. I'll call it a sort of shift or absorption of wisdom for want of a better term. Have I said enough to qualify for a padded cell on the hill yet?"

"Honestly, not at all. Some call it self-realization."

"Understand me, Basil, I'm not expecting you to buy into such intoxicating thoughts. All I ask is that you allow me to embrace them."

"I have no objection to your intimacy with the dunes. Their validity is within you. You know, I'm new to this dune thing. I'll affirm here and now that you are of sound mind and I'm sincerely taken with it all. After all, you seem to have found a special source of inner peace."

"You noticed that, Basil?"

"Of course. Seeking inner peace remains my quotidian haunt. Getting there and maintaining it seems to be the problem. My hunch is that everyone desires inner peace, something humanly intrinsic. May I go to my next question, Suzanne?"

"Please do."

"We're on the same page, Suzanne. Would you tell me what your current ambition is? You mentioned it before."

"Yes, I'll tell you. I'll make this short but not especially sweet. My plan is to seek ways for all of us to find lasting inner peace and to be able to show myself and possibly others how to overcome the stresses so very many of us are entangled in. I mean those real or imagined barriers of the kind that hold us captive. I'm speaking of a wide range in more depth then the simplistic ones like the advice to the lovelorn in news columns."

"I'll tell you right now, Suzanne, the key words in your soliloquy is your penchant to hold fast to realism without the usual touchy-feely trappings. The next question is how?"

"Do you think people might find this helpful?"

"Of course. Why not?"

"Tell me, Basil, I like to listen. Why?"

"Your '*Why*' is like some sort of a Zen-Buddhist riddle, a tricky koan, Suzanne."

"No. I seek something solvable. Since you ask, then why do we seem to have thoughts as we do? The answer evades me, although I have an analogy; I seem to have some guidance when I make a declaration. Do you remember when we were learning to write? My teacher, Miss Spooner, would cover my hand in hers and guide mine to form the letters correctly."

"Yup. I guess most of us needed that help. You know something, sweetie, we are delving into some heavy stuff. I confess these questions have occurred to me."

"Perhaps you and I and maybe everyone else has something inside demanding those answers. Are we devoid of answers?" Suzanne asked.

"Well, here we are. If you put together anything that would come close to helping people attain inner peace in this menagerie called civilization you could relieve so many of us - help us unload the burdens that I know you're alluding to."

"I wouldn't presume to know the answers. I think maybe that is why we're here. You understand me? Is it not somewhat unusual the way we met and then the questions we have and the similarity of our interests?"

"Shucks sweetie, I've thought of it as a happy convergence of events! Where else could a guy find an idyllic vacation spot and a lovely girl, a graduate of philosophy and religion, living next door. Might happen anywhere, but it does give one cause to wonder."

"I don't know about this preordained stuff; but it's way ahead of you know what."

"I know what Suzanne: shit-luck. We have the interest and time to at least make a dent in this stuff. You've paralleled something asked by Nietzsche, I think I've got it; '*Who are we*', and; '*The truth is that we remain strangers to ourselves.*'"

"Hey you! Please recall that I'm the philosophic major here, but I acknowledge that you've hit the nail squarely."

"You've done great so far. You've pulled the sheets back on a devilishly haunting question. Are you willing to go the extra mile to extract these hidden secrets of life? Really Suzanne, you've alluded to these matters so much!"

"I'm beyond alluding, Basil. Let me show you. I wrote something once; it's in my laptop. Let me read it:"

LIVING IN THE MOMENT

The moment is the present, that time of the now.
A time that may require looking back and forward,
especially to look at our lives in depth and to note
the many areas of freedom and devotion that we share.
We believers have succeeded in extending a mutuality
of freedom and action in the Spiritual and the secular.
The freedom to worship where and how we wish and even beyond;
That freedom to believe as we wish, our souls guidance,
something denied to many.
We give our love and understanding to all sentient beings.
We cherish our prose and poetry and occasionally
express opinion in our local papers.
We return the unconditional love of our family pets
who nearly close the common divide.
We have meaningfulness in life. We have taken the step
to embrace our love to all and our oneness in man.
We respect the lessons given by those who have gone before.
We acknowledge the madness of our world,
and our collective responsibility for its inhumanity.
We pursue those small acts of charity and love as we are able
as we walk a path to the mountain summit.

"You reached me with that. I sense a new beginning. You are not bound by tradition, of that I'm sure. You've closed the gap. I've fought the battle, like I said, since I was a teenager. I succeeded in dumping all the extraneous stuff and some of the rest, but you know what?"

"Yes, I do know what! You're the hollow man; you've dismissed and rejected all that stuff, but you failed in your attempt to find what you really are. Don't hate me, Basil, for I'm still searching too."

"I don't hate you, but my ego just fell on a rock pile."

"Let me tell you of a philosopher named Joseph Ernest Renan, a French philosopher of great repute. Let me read from my laptop. He said:

'There are many chances that the world may be nothing but a fairy pantomime of which no God has care. We must therefore arrange ourselves so that on neither hypothesis we shall be completely wrong. We must listen to the superior voices, but in such a way that if the second hypothesis were true we should not have been too completely duped. If in fact the world be not a serious thing, it is the dogmatic people who will be the shallow ones, and the worldly minded whom the theologians now call frivolous will be those who are really wise. In Utrumque paratus, then. Be ready for anything-that perhaps is wisdom. Give ourselves up, according to the hour, to confidence, to skepticism, to optimism, to irony, and we may be sure that at certain moments at least we shall be with the truth.....'
We owe it to the Eternal to be virtuous; but we have the right to add to this tribute our irony as a sort of personal reprisal. In this way we return to the right quarter jest for jest; we play the trick that has been played on us. St. Augustine's phrase; Lord, if we are deceived, it is by thee! Remains a fine one, well suited to our modern feeling.'

"Is this where you are my dear friend? Have you hedged your bets? Was the promise hedged in with so many ifs and buts that you couldn't rely on it. Stomp on that ego for a moment!"

"I don't know. Sometimes I think my soul is fired up for some unknown," he replied.

"Aha, your soul! And perhaps your God has prepared a place at table and awaits. Your soul may be like your brain; a sponge waiting for satiation."

"Please, Suzanne! I'm opening up to you because you understand. I know I'm outside the mainstream. I've a bunch of ideas like I told you, but my head is a jumble of porridge."

"Think for a moment. Are you actually outside the main stream? Don't you know that others carry the same questions around? Don't be pseudo modern. You can clean up your mind, like; '*you got chaff*?' Discard the chaff like they do with a computer; you know: Delete, delete, delete!"

"You're suggesting that I defrag the hard drive of my being; Is that it?"

"Yeah, that might work. Clean it up."

"Now I have a *yes-but*; '*Defragging My Soul*' sounds like a song title!"

"How about this, Basil; suppose we widen that field and write something together. We might call it:

DEFRAGGING ONE'S BEING.

We might get on the main track and reach those others loaded with baggage."

"I'll go with unloading the baggage, and I like your train analogy; just offload the chaff at the next station platform and away it blows."

"Basil, my thought is this; we're fresh. Our academics are in top shape, we're ready, but for what? This could be that fork in the road!"

"Yes, I recall. You speak of Yogi Berra's wisdom: '*When you come to a fork in the road- take it!* ' I hear you! We've met, we've consumed, we haven't screwed, nor have we killed one another! We're a credit to our Homosapiens' way! And I add, we've found a common purpose haven't we? I've been grasping all along but nothing ever came from it until today. Now tell me; just what is your idea of the way to approach this burning in our minds?"

"You may have created a maxim, Basil. Rather than wrestle with my opinion we might visit the historical side and examine the philosophers, those enlightened ones may still provide the answers to; *'Where's the beef?'*"

"You want to hear mine? Where's the beef! I'll tell you. My big beef is simple; Why the war? We've had about two thousand years of Christian ideals, but rather than the return of the Messiah, the nations find war to be their pastime of choice."

"Oh, my dear Basil, it's a test of reality, in peace we prepare for war and a profound uncertainty is in all of us."

"A very small percentage of our population is involved in these wars. So few of us look war directly in the eye. Don't you think that those of us who for whatever reason don't fight the wars are getting away easy? Our propaganda system is the soothing anodyne."

"Not soothing enough. A very small minority of us have someone in the military; and like me, I care, but it's all so distant, so far from my being."

"But Suzanne, like any of us, you can give lip service, wave the flag of patriotism, put a decal on your car saying *'We support our troops.'*"

"War has always been like this hasn't it?"

"I guess. A favorite and ancient Chinese poet named Tu Fu of Chang-an wrote during a time of revolution and war:

> *'Last night a government order came*
> *To enlist boys who had reached eighteen*
> *They must help defend the capital*
> *O Mother! O children, do not weep so!*
> *Shedding such tears shall injure you*
> *When tears stop flowing then bones come through,*
> *Nor heaven nor earth has compassion then..'*

"There's such a touch of authentic humanism by him. You've certainly read some poetry, Basil. It reminds me of something that a man wrote who in my opinion was a great philosopher. It was Voltaire who asked:

> *'I want to know what were the steps by which*
> *men passed from barbarism to civilization.'*

"That only he should live today, what would he say, Suzanne?"

"Voltaire lived at times in an era called *'bubbles of peace'* just as we sometimes think we do and to me his inquiry was very tongue in cheek."

"Indeed, it probably was. I concur, but do you see why my refusal to accept some claims as absolute is the very reason I'm not a firm adherent to much at all. It seems to exist in everyone's culture, a dominant school of thought. I recall a popular statement from not long ago, that *'There has to be a war every twenty years or so.'* Think of this; how many like me abandon their attempts in seeking to secure well founded beliefs because of staggering questions about the admonitions of timeless validity and compromised thoughts? I've thought of my life as an illusion, a fashionable unreality. A fellow named Sun Tsu wrote the book on strategies of war. I wrote an editorial to my local paper one day when our nation got involved in Afghanistan."

"I'll bet you carry it around, too," said Suzanne.

"I do. At the time there was a flurry of books hitting the market about war. My response was in regard to those books:

The sudden preoccupation with books of war in D.C. is too little and too late. Although political science does not illuminate the path to the future, the adage that 'those who forget history are bound to repeat it' remains valid.

That the world is driven by history is no indicator that the next war will be like any other. Vietnam is not Afghanistan. Protecting colonial interests in

Vietnam and the red scare cost our side over 58000 souls. What a historical error!

The book readers in D.C. might sharpen their skills by reading The Art of War by Sun Tzu, a valuable primer that is as true today as it was 2,500 years ago. Among Barbara Tuchman's contributions, The March of Folly is a classic addressing war from Troy to Vietnam. Book reading is fine, but never forget, America's young men are in war's crosshairs.'

"Oh, Basil, I understand what you wrote. To me, the rogue tyrants who lead us to war are utilizing an age old SOP, Simply: *'Provide the masses with a cause to hate some perceived enemy; introduce a large dose of fear; add the threat of inherent danger and provide an undercurrent of hidden propaganda and some likely intrigue.'* Those are the ingredients to raise the populace to go to war."

"You baked the biscuits with that one, Suzanne."

"What you've said admits light to the hanging questions from so many sources in life, but it lacks resolution."

"I'll put it on the line then. Those hanging questions that razzle dazzle my mind are basic to civilization. Stop me if I'm wrong, Suzanne, but in my studies I found that throughout the ages that war is the prevailing controller of mankind."

"Nah. To my thinking it's domination. Consider Christianity or any religion; A majority of its adherents are drawn into supporting the warring actions of their nation. The ordinary person supporting the patriotism of his nation thinks of it as noble, lofty and mandatory and that its values are absolute. The mind approves of the absolute perspective of patriotic-religion; the nation remains held in an aura of the sacred. Religions are easily captured within this national sentiment, where religion and patriotism unite. Super-nationalism gathers strength in that religion oftentimes finds its culture and interests parallel that of national groups. I found in my studies of religion that the opening lines of Romans 13:1-7 has been used to justify military oppression:

> *Let every person be subject to the governing authorities*
> *for there is no authority except from God, and those*
> *authorities that exist have been instituted by God.*
> *Therefore whoever resists authority resists what God has*
> *appointed and those who resist will incur judgment.*

"I remember back when our nation invaded Iraq that some evangelical preachers used the passage you referenced to legitimize and support the military action, and in Germany before WW II, many of the German Christians embraced this passage to justify their devotion to the Third Reich, defending its culture and supporting an attribute of universality."

"Yes, Basil, but the law of unintended consequences overtook the axis powers causing their failure. Must people always assume that God is marching with them into battle?"

"It may also be conformity that plays a large part. Speaking of conformity or the lack of it, take a look at this paper. I wrote it a while back. It defines my overall position pretty well:"

I'm more than a little envious of the life-style of Henry David Thoreau, whose stay at Walden Pond epitomizes what some of us might emulate providing one could live as he did in today's world. Thoreau enjoyed a huge degree of freedom that few have enjoyed in any century. His life was that of a non-conformist and a rare exception in that he didn't miss the mark of defining our nation's non-compliant mode. His belief in the occasional necessity of acts of civil disobedience accompanied by his call for freedom and the rights of man has not been lost on our citizens. Indeed, one can declare Thoreau's attitude to be safely engrained in our collective intellect. I believe it's a majority. We aspire to his quality of freedom and expression without limit, ranging from the disenfranchised, of the homeless and run the entire gamut to military veterans and to all citizens who subscribe to the definition of Patriot.

In short, it is time to scratch the itch; to be absolutists in our demand that our national freedom extends to all, and to assure that no one's rights are abrogated. Recent challenges to our culture and way of life demand that we examine closely what is driving our lives and our long range aspirations. I'm sure that Thoreau would have been seriously troubled about the U.S attack on Iraq. What has begun as a possibly short term war has escalated to over nine years. The middle east has taken the lives of thousands of our military, many more with injuries both short term and life long. The losses of life in Iraq alone are said to be in excess of 500000. Now we are placing our aggression on a time table, the assurance that it will be over by 2014. How convenient! Game over. Really?

We are a warring nation. This has been shown in Korea, Panama, Vietnam, Granada, Iraq & Afghanistan. We traded 58000 lives and deliberately devastated South Vietnam. And by the way, The United States hasn't won a war since WWII.

Israel is our puppet state in the middle east. Does anyone actually believe that the U.S. Government wants Palestine and Israel to find peace. No, because then the Israelis would be aligned with the middle east countries.

Our country has replaced domination by superior manufacturing and ability to conduct commerce by the threats of force. This is a dangerous road to travel. A pretty much ignored reason is our educational system. It has essentially failed our youth. Our infrastructure requires substantial improvement. The money is going to war materials and interest payments. We, as the citizens on the street are being fed a trickle down propaganda system with the media in lockstep with what we are to believe and support. Our dissonance at the governmental level remains under the scrutiny of internationalists who wait and watch. Does anyone else think that many influences in life are other than objective cognitive thought. Yup, I thought so. There seems to be certain suggestive grabbers out there today. It's more than groupthink. It' approaches mind poisoning. We must do more than writhe in the agony of job loss, and foreclosure and business failure. Citizens must be vocal at all levels. Worthy of discussion. Yes! Oh Henry Thoreau where are you? I've been itching to tell you, but of course I had to wait – what for?, Well, to scratch the itch. At the risk of redundancy, I warn you now, your earth may rotate at warp speed.' Basil Porter

"Oh, Basil! You're seeking to find why the failures of peace and unanimity occur."

"Oh yes!" Can you think of a better reason to write? Of course, we can write it off to the so-called '*nature of man,*' that's easy, but then we regress to living in a theater of illusion."

"Basil, you're treading close to my interests; I've never believed that war and its horrors to be the nature of man. I'm talking religion and philosophy and I think your next question is: '*Why have the great teachings failed?*'"

"Your question fits well into my theory of why - yeah, why do we seemingly open the door to another bout of a world at war, by declaring it's all for defense and peace?"

"You've got the ball, Basil. Run with it!"

"O.K. Consider Constantine's epiphany at Milvian Bridge. His return from successful battle to become a forceful leader of Rome was engineered essentially by Eusebius. Constantine's vision of the cross led to Christianization of the shield; Onward Christian soldiers. He also became a beloved leader of the Christians, initiating a cause and effect, a turning point where in a natural manner the Christians embraced his ideology both politically and militarily. This initiated the synthesis of Christendom in Rome."

"I know, Constantine pulled their chestnuts out of the fire."

"Indeed, he very likely saved Christendom from the ravages of a harassing and unfriendly society and the possible termination of that newfound religion. Constantine provided houses of worship, tax exemptions, along with assistance in building the beginnings of the Church, but there is one major factor that is contrary to the teachings of Jesus. The acceptance of war as a necessity of man. Now do you get it?"

"I do. We're speaking of a conjoined pair of opposites irredeemable and to this day inseparable."

"Isn't it strange, Suzanne, that as we speak in terms of good wars and bad wars that the carnage continues, the forces of evil march on with little objection by the Christian constituency."

"It's called necessity; defense, us or them."

"Now that's getting to the main thrust of my argument. That term *just war*, that endorsement by religionists of lawful killing, that failure of the power of circumscription to condemn war is the green light, the enabler by which new wars are initiated. Also, the precept exists that every man ought to endeavor for peace, as far as the hope of obtaining it is concerned, but if this is impossible, that he may seek to use all means to defend himself. I must state from the gitgo that certain of men seek war for advantage, not defense. Herein is a cause and effect situation. The part saying that man should employ all means to defend himself accentuates the likelihood of war. A fearful competitiveness occurs wherein a buildup to war is inevitable. This is the primary fatal mistake. In our contemporary world, the desire for war is said to address some grievance whether by a nation, nationality, religious belief, tribe or even an individual."

"Do you feel that a gradual decline in man's desire for peace has occurred?"

"It's immeasurable, Suzanne. Who could qualify to know the hearts of men over the ages to confirm or deny. A subjective opinion might say a trend exists within the world's mandarin class to encourage self-serving war. A despot anticipating a wargasm can't hardly wait for the curtain to go up. What I would like is that a new rationale to induce creditable and praiseworthy ideals of world peace is confirmed."

"One key is to convince leaders that war is futile."

"The availability of WMD is a deterrent of retaliation. Isn't it strange that the threat of death has more affect then all the peace talks?"

"Perhaps the nature of man is revealed, that insidious fear of death."

"Suzanne; I'm a little scared of this. This is audacious to the nth degree. Our audacity could cause us to figuratively swing in the wind, or worse."

"You're the mathematician. Maybe you can generate some statistics on how likely we'll hang in someone's village square. The time is ripe. Like Nixon said, '*Seize the moment!* And you said, Basil; what better reason than the timeliness of now?"

"Perhaps timeliness is upon us."

Suzanne drove on our return from the dunes. It was otherwise uneventful. Suzanne said; "You look exhausted." She was right. Then she poked a little fun at me;

"I've got one for you, Oh great swami: Were the lions on Noah's Ark vegetarians?"

Just before Basil dozed off he answered, "Genetic engineering wasn't available at the time. Conversion to herbivores may have eased the anxiety of some passengers."

⊷╬╪⊶

A driving rain sought to permeate the cottages all night . Basil saw light in Suzanne's windows in the early hours. Soon after he dashed through the stinging downpour to her door balancing a carafe of fresh-brewed coffee.

"Come in quick," said Suzanne holding the door with an extended arm.

"What a rain!" Basil rolled raindrops from his cap and slid into a chair at the kitchen table.

"Finish cooking our breakfast, would you, Basil? I want to get dressed."

"Sure will," Basil followed her departure. Rather than bask in eroticism he checked his thoughts to rethink those of yesterday.

Suzanne returned, "You've burned the biscuits, you naughty boy!"

"I was thinking."

Suzanne kissed him tenderly. "You're forgiven."

Basil said, "If it isn't too early, I want to ask, just where are we going with all this conversation from the other day?"

"Well, neither peace on earth nor love of mankind is a new concept, yet their implementation has been evasive, don't you agree?"

"Aha, exactly my point! If I may pursue another question, Suzanne. Should we not simply accept the status quo. We could travel the world speaking of peace and love and yet to borrow from street talk, our tiny influence is '*a piss-hole in the snow!*'"

"Now Basil! You were so positive yesterday, saying; '*what better to write about*' so let's stop the negativism. Why not review some political science to see if man's atavism has recurred. We might narrow things down, like discover where mankind went off the tracks."

"Your comment of a worldwide train wreck is on target. Are we actually up to it; you know, telling it like it is?"

"I don't know of many attempts, at least in recent times and anyway, who's to judge our qualifications?"

"To employ your train idiom, we could jolly well find out at the end of the line!"

"It's going to rain all day. This is a good time to start. Say yes!"

"Yes. I have something to toss into the ring this instant. I'm wondering if the multitudinous inputs arriving in our information age is reshaping everyone's thinking?"

"I'll venture that we could be floundering around without its benefits. Anyway, is anyone able to really absorb our chameleonic culture?"

"Aha, you're asking whether mankind can handle these cultural changes."

"Yup, that's it. When we lived isolated in our own little worlds major happenings mightn't ever reach us and if they did the elapsed time destined them to the history bin."

"You're saying if we read it, watch it or hear it, then our individual system has received it. Now it's in the works awaiting whatever resolution we decide."

"Exactly Basil. Your insight is right on. I mean some information is internalized for better or for worse," Suzanne couldn't restrain her laughter.

"Alright. Is it fair to say we as a people are constantly absorbing these wearing inputs with affects on our culture and our value system?"

I'm recognizing a frightening potential result of our own making, Basil. You said value system. That's a relevant factor and deserves consideration. This conversation is leading up to a contempt for humanity."

"How so?"

"Simply that we are despising in others what exists in ourselves."

"You're saying we're like migratory locusts who consume, screw and kill and we're the same! Would you color that hypocritical?"

"I'm saying that self deception and vanity make the hypocrite."

"This brings me to a conclusion; namely our culture and ethics are influenced and undermined for example by the suggestibility of the evening news. It's possible that our standards are softened up and lands us in a gradual acceptance of throwback morality. Remember Suzanne, when we only wanted to examine the thoughts of some of our philosophers and spiritual leaders?"

"Of course. Few, if any, anticipated this threat to civilization, the eventual mass extinction from those potentials we fear today."

"Here's a poser. Will civilization as we know it end by reason of war or will we terminate via earthbound tellurian asteroid, or - one more please- shall we just exhaust the resources necessary to support humanity and collapse in a failed global bio-diversity?"

"There'll be no second guessing, Basil. Two of them are within man's comprehension but questionably within man's control. Your asteroid strike is a nebulae. Dust unto dust. If you think of man's presence on earth as a flash in the pan of time, then we're only another species pushed aside by the great bulldozer of death. Do you like my answer?"

"Would anyone? Perhaps we are the locusts. Wars throughout history have been over land acquisition and the control of resources including people. I agree that man might control two of the three. We're looking the four horsemen of the apocalypse squarely in the eyes! *Avarice, war, famine and pestilence.* You get it yet?"

"How can I escape your meaning, Basil? You didn't use *death personified* though; you used avarice."

"You're asking me why? I'll tell you. Avarice defined is an insatiable desire for wealth and its concomitant; power. To me the shoe fits."

"I think you're saying that avarice leads to death; like evil, it carries the seed of its own destruction."

"That's my take on it. Wouldn't you concur that avarice is often the forerunner of the three remaining?"

"You know, Basil, that's not bad for a political science and mathematics major."

"It's about lunchtime. Let's eat. I left fish in my fridge yesterday. I'll go get it."

They ate silently and after finishing up Suzanne spoke directly.

⚊⬩⬩⚊

"The term avarice seems so all inclusive, not at all confined to wealth but rather a road to power. Seems to me we're topping out on some structured *Gomorrah-like* place notorious for vice and corruption."

"I think you've got it, Suzanne! Can you think of one?"

"Are you kidding? I can recall what I read; the triumphant oligarchy of rich men. But, you know what?"

"I bet I can't guess."

"You're a little facetious Basil. You know very well; I'm speaking of the limits and of course there are none."

"Most readings of the *nature of man* will confirm your statement."

"Are you quite sure of that? Among my studies I discovered something that contradicts that. Meister Eckhart said: *'By nature every creature seeks to become like God. Nature's intent is neither food nor drink, not clothing nor comfort, not anything else in which God is left out. Whether you like it or not, secretly nature seeks, hunts, tries to ferret out the track on which God may be found.'"*

"Well, since you seek extremes, Bertrand Russell said: *'The secret of happiness is to face the fact that the world is horrible, horrible, horrible.'* and I will mention his shared writings, Principia Mathematica, with Alfred North Whitehead, which to me shows the logic of a singularly massive contribution. The writings of the *nature of man* is right on target for us. I found that my abrupt refusal to get in line with the culture somewhat paralleled Wilhelm Nietzsche's opinion of man's advent of the ascetic ideal. He said something like: *'Man overcame his weakness as a plaything of circumstance, a will-of-the wisp, and obtained a will: the power to make decisions; but with its inclusive accessories: a hatred of humanity, loathing of the senses, fear of beauty and happiness, longing to escape illusion, change, becoming, reason and death. The nature of man; a will to nothingness, revulsion of life, rebellion of living.'*"

"Surely, Basil, you don't support that view!"

"The will-yes. Here's the but: The will package contains options. An awakening to the world of science and philosophy needled civilization to look again at their limited exercise of the will. There became in the minds of many a converging of science and philosophy, but not a happy one because of man's existent belief of infinite concern - that of religion, especially emphasis within the church. On the one hand, during a time of unexcelled church attendance there occurred a marginalization of religion, a surrendering of the old values. A complacency occurred, a kind of giving over to the governments the rights war, an absence of the will, a leaning to a conformist culture and massive consumption, Mankind holds only a modicum of control of our own narrative. Does our modern era suggest the need of a changed integration of church and society?"

"Without a doubt. The acceptance or rejection of sweeping social attitudes and the inclusion of subjects of former absolute anathema within the churches such as gaiety, same-sex marriage to name two has produced a further distancing of the secular and religious. The religious conscience is being sharply tweaked, especially affecting the conservative churches. An attitude of scorn and opprobrium exists today, one that is not given to negotiation," said Suzanne.

"I wonder," ventured Basil, "whether Nietzsche's proposal of employing a healing interaction utilizing his Apollonian and Dionysian intervention might reveal a path to reconciliation of a matter otherwise insoluble as viewed today."

"No. Resolution is not so easily at hand. One can read of various church denominations falling like dominoes to the inclination of permissiveness and total acceptance of homosexuality, a complete capitulation from earlier convictions; that of many a position of strict adherence to the rule of God as believed and perpetuated in the past."

"What you've said, Suzanne, is that the church of conservative Christians will likely remain to their belief that the human body is a temple to the Holy Spirit, unchangeable and indefatigable. Not within the auspices of subjectivity.

"So, are we sliding down the slippery banks to Gomorrah?"

"Apparently not in the eyes of the millions whose freedom of will has no existing prohibitions."

"I have an opinion which I think is germane to the big picture. I'll restrict my comment to those many variations of Christianity commonly called denominations. The denominations have within each structure the elements of belief, methods of worship and so forth. I note that these several discrete sets impose certain beliefs to be adhered to by their constituent membership. Was not the existence of each denomination predicated on the desired beliefs of their founders?

"Of course, Suzanne."

"And haven't modifications been enacted over the years by those entrusted with matters of the denomination?"

"Yes."

'Then the implementation by a denomination to endorse the *Open and Affirming* option is a valid one."

"So, where's the beef?"

"My point exactly. I'm reminded of something Voltaire said: *'Opinion governs the world, but it is the wise who ultimately govern opinion.'*"

※

"People don't change. Conscience guided people were deceived by the seductive disguises of evil back then. Unfortunately a tendency exists for many to accept a modified conscience instead of a clear conscience. Those of the intellectually elite, often people in power, expect the general populace to follow the folly rather than to exercise their wisdom and independence of mind."

"What I'm hearing, Basil, is a thinly veiled suggestion describing the nature of some of our leaders or at least an insinuation that they or their cohorts are prone to favor legislation serving financial interests or favorite prejudices."

"I'm saying the *Lilly-Path* can be a slippery slope. A status hierarchy of the intelligentsia who have the power to enact laws to control or discourage the perpetuation by others to influence Congress or vote to seek to remove from office those who exercise inequality as the law of the land. I'm only demonstrating a trend; the exercise of which permits financial power to subjugate others. Look at today; have you noticed the *'bought and paid for'* influence on specific legislations?"

"That's what we're doing isn't it, Basil?"

"We are now. I feel a strong connection like from this moment on we might team up and write a useful book, not the abysmal do-goody touchy feely stuff."

"Gosh, Suzanne, this is so close to what I've had in mind to write on this summer. What about us getting into double harness to serve the current milieu.

"Oh yes, I almost forgot the milieu. Tell you what, you don't say milieu and I won't berate your double harness with my buggy whip. What we really need is a strong suggestive guidance, one that demonstrates ways for anyone to extract the negativism in their existence."

"You're saying we're destined to provide the keys for anyone, including us, to adopt and maintain a robust permanent peak experience within no matter what negatives are in play?"

"That's close enough, Basil. Like the small print usually says; 'certain conditions apply!' 'One is that everyone must accept responsibility for their acts. One must attempt to live within the laws expressed in their current society, respecting the customary rules, even those of repressive propriety, except when change must occur."

"That could raise some hackles in some of us, Suzanne. That places restraints on the principal of free will, does it not? Would your plan mean that a person could not challenge society to force change? I'm thinking of nowadays, the legalizing of recreational marijuana, ending incarceration of political prisoners in Guantanamo, the conflict of governmental abortion laws', and we must prohibit laws designed to limit or control any person's rights to vote. I could go on."

"You're saying that respecting repressive laws raise hackles because they shackle! I think you know better than to suggest that I would in anyway want to restrict or limit people's rights. And by the way, your mention of those specifics lead me to explain one of the problems we face."

"And what exactly is that?"

"Devotion to the status quo. You know, samo-samo; otherwise known as existence bias. It's a fixation assuming that nothing can be done to bring about change. My example is the laws enacted to punish individuals possessing drugs. Some of the sentences imposed will outlive the defendants. I'm talking the frustration many face by the force of law and the delay to institute change."

"A political action committee may serve you better than offering advice on how to overcome negativism."

"First, Basil, it's important to position yourself sufficiently to attempt to make changes. To get out of the rut first, and then I wouldn't rule out political action by those displeased with current conditions. Let me explain something; most of us watch T.V. and catch the evening news, or read a newspaper or news mags. Some T.V. shows are designed to push a political agenda. News is often contaminated at its source, or at an editor's discretion, some of which is more disingenuous than a Hollywood air-kiss. Magazines are frequently propaganda driven organs. Motion pictures so often espouse the current daring to titillate or condone violence."

Suzanne continued, "The purpose of propagandized information is to bend the minds to concur with an agenda. Now, here's a question for you. Don't you think that a citizen watching political media games may become disillusioned, and even develop anxieties upon recognizing the snow job they're getting? Does the obvious impact of the show's influence generate a suspicion about the intent of those producing it? Can you agree that those who recognize the unsubtle intent to manipulate data and suppress conflicting views may even develop a neuroses, caused by a desire to reject rather than acquiesce to the propaganda of the programmer?"

"In a word, yes," said Basil, "I would remind you that the freedom granted in this country still includes freedom of the press and all variations of informational matter. We must respect the freedom of opinion of those we disagree with, otherwise we don't respect freedom of expression at all. That said, your point about one who recognizes the absence of truth accompanied by a heavy coat of delusional jingoism and subliminal allegations may be swimming in the rubbish of attempted mind control of the masses."

"I want to begin by stating that propaganda wasn't always a pejorative term, but language games create an element that I find distressing. The purpose of propaganda today is to disguise the obvious, to offer up mythical goals, and hide the true purposes of those in power."

"Gotcha, Suzanne. Submissiveness can be exploited. A submissive sheep is a find for a wolf. I think a good workaround is better, rather than to accept whatever is dished out for public consumption by the media. We can attempt to extract those facts, the raisins in the pudding being served, though it may be a difficult task."

⊷⊶

"You had more to say Basil. Where is it?"

"I was hoping you'd forgotten. I was sixteen and had just got my driver's license. I was rapidly approaching the definition of an upstart radical. I was hot on the issue of our President's speaking of us as a *Christian Nation*. To me his statement is subjective, although understandably acceptable by many. Our country embraces freedom of religion. His indifference placed other religions as nationally inexistent."

"He was likely only playing up to the majority to gain support for his war."

"Chances are. I also found that our incidental support of colonialism lead to U.S. troops engaging in war, a number of closely related incidences since W.W. II. I saw no relation to Christianity or any other religion as I understand them."

"So, is that it? The majority of clergy have implicitly concurred with these wars by a noticeable absence of opposition, although we've heard from several of the clergy and a slew of others who have opposed these wars of recent memory."

"No, that isn't all. I have great respect for those who opposed recent wars, and also those who have served our nation as well. But, there's more."

"I think I know where you're going. It's something left over from the early days, the ones you described as your thicket of questionable beliefs, like you said, dogma, and all those establishment facts, and socially acceptable clichés."

"Of course that's it. I decided to take my leave from the church where I'd grown up."

"You're not the only one who has done that."

"Well, like others, I found reasons to drop from the Christian fold."

"Sounds like your faith experienced a negative tumescence like George Costanza's discovery after swimming in a cold pool."

"Au contraire, mine wasn't from any inadequacy. I wasn't able to support those axiomatic claims from the testaments in the light of my own pragmatism. I found that I had to apply provisional truth to much of it."

"Oh, Basil, truth is provisional. Boredom, was that it too?"

"Yes, I'm certain of that. My experience was a sleepy one. I joined those in the congregation who fought sleep. Perhaps it's a lack of intellectual stimulation."

"Well, well! You bailed didn't you. Any regrets?"

"Thought you might ask. I had time to think after I left the Church. I used most of it internalizing and building support of my ideas."

"Are you saying you had some sort of epiphany, Basil."

"Sort of. Over time I recognized the good influence of both religion and that of several philosophers and believe me, if you want to call it revelation or epiphany it struck pretty hard."

"Of course. Then you engaged in a sort of semi-spiritual masturbation," Suzanne replied laughingly.

"I'm not sure I'd call it that. It was an epiphany of a new consciousness; that's what. I had taken to reading a lot about the worlds religions when a slowly evolving thought occurred to me. It was an eye-opener. Basically, I realized that even considering all the faults and fault-finders, the religions' integral is the power for good. I found the influence of the Hindi and Buddhists to be good."

"So tell me, what's the problem?"

"You really want to hear my whole story, Suzanne?"

"Yup. If I fall asleep you can wake me."

"Thanks for the humor. We'll need some for this. Do you know what came into play here, Suzanne?"

"I'll bet my bikini it's the elimination of war among nations."

"You win. Keep it on. Now, I'll begin. Existent wrongs can be rectified. A tolerant and peace seeking people of any creed can move to avoid the actuality of war by employing negotiation rather than strong arm methods. You may ask how does the direction of peace becomes real; where is the path to peace for an aggrieved people?"

"I think you're onto it Basil."

"Of course I am, and the reasoned solution employs the will of any people who are organized to maintain peace through their religious convictions."

"Big question! I ask you, why religious convictions? "Wars are fought over these convictions."

"The answer is in the strength of leadership within the convictions of religion and belief. All the religions and beliefs I know of are on their surface peace loving. We have had our excursions into war where religion as well as political and the acquisition of real estate with its concomitant value have been the primary reasons. It is time to move past that. The annihilation of civilization as we know it is possibly the next step in war. To answer your question, I ask you; what else exists today that has the barest chance of preventing war? Governments come and go, entire civilizations exist and then fade away. Beliefs in a supreme being is one positive element that remain an influence. The credibility of those beliefs isn't in question. The actualization of them by the believers themselves is what mankind has to save itself from war."

"You've made a convincing argument, Basil. If I'm still a part of this effort, may I suggest we eat before hunger overcomes us both?"

"I'm sorry, I've taken up too much time. Tell you what, I'll spring for dinner, but it's my choice, somewhere *'Down-Cape'* tonight?"

"How can I refuse Are we traveling via-Harley tonight?'

"Let's try it. You might like it."

⊶≒⊷ ⊶≒⊷

"Let's order now. I want to get on with my story," said Basil.

"Go on. I love eating on this deck with the sunset over the water."

"The military-industrial establishment in the United States has a symbiotic relationship with its political policies. one that finds by-passes to military aggression."

"Are you suggesting that we base any decision to go to war on a ballot question or turn our war decisions over to the clergy?"

"No Suzanne, not at all. I am suggesting that our clergy develop a constituency, speak ex cathedra to members of their folds who I hope would actively oppose war."

Suzanne spoke, "Contrary to Emerson's saying, '*as men's prayers are a disease of the will, so are their creeds a disease of the intellect,*' *we* haven't yet entered the phase called a post-Christian world, nor are we a post-Christian nation, Basil, but we are toying with the destruction of our universe. There seems to be a parallel in the *Wizard of Oz*. The wizard is seen by those fascinating travelers from the yellow brick road and he declares: '*Pay no attention to that man*' . Our '*wizards*' are military strategists and those planning our advanced weapons. Our yellow brick road can lead to oblivion. We can become the doomed conformists, the human equivalent of the mythical lemmings who follow one another to the sea and drown. Our alternative is to control the actions of those despots whose conscience isn't concerned with the loss of the youth of our nation sent to fight their real or imagined enemy."

"Now, Suzanne, we're on the same page. Here's my take on it; The United States is now paralleling ancient Rome more today than when Oliver Wendell Holmes stated that; '*We are the Romans of the modern world-the great assimilating people, Conflicts and conquests are with us, as with our prototypes.*'"

"You're speaking of our invasion of Iraq of course." said Suzanne.

"By no means limited to Iraq. After WWII, our nation became by far the most dominant world wide power and we have used that power during the last seventy years or so to build a worldwide hegemony.

During the time of the Roman Empire, the Imperial theology was in Caesar the Imperator. The U.S. today is predominately of the Christian faith."

"It would seem that after the time of Constantine's conversion to Christianity that the desire for everlasting peace would have penetrated throughout the Roman Empire, as I often thought, but Constantine was a warrior and had tasted the blood of victory in the past. Could Constantine's conversion to Christianity have inadvertently caused a reduction in the love spirit of the early Christian community?" asked Suzanne.

"War became inevitable with the discussions of *just-war* becoming the gateway to ongoing conflicts by the Romans," replied Basil.

"I've heard of *just-war'*. Is it not now used today to obtain official sanction to initiate war?" asked Suzanne.

"Right on Suzanne; this gets me right to the place that I think would be a great introductory chapter in our proposed book."

"And what would that be, oh great sage?"

"I'm not really sure of the best place to begin, but what do you think of something I would call *Historicity's extended trauma?*"

"I love it, Basil. Explain to me please."

"Well, here goes. What I mean by history's extended trauma is the frequent reminders of Nazism and the horrors of the second world war, with all the nuances that historians and denying revisionists can re-think to keep our minds churning with oft repeated stories and the addition of new findings or falsified interpretations."

"Your intent is to reduce the trauma of repetition?"

"Simply that most of us, even those of the so-called younger generations, have been thoroughly indoctrinated in the stories of WWII with an overkill of much of it. It isn't that we shouldn't be informed and it is something never to forget, but that these constant inputs and reminders place a strain on those who've had the subject drilled into their heads, some for generations." he said.

"The result?"

"A building of stress caused by repeated inputs of the horrors of it all, leading to a kind of quasi acceptance of war's violence and a need to find relief from its unceasing indoctrination."

"I think the constant stirring of the bones of WWII are what disturb me the most, especially the Holocaust, the Pearl Harbor attack, the decision about Hiroshima and Nagasaki. Not only those, but we are constantly forced to relive on the screen and the news all the horrors along with details of Korea, Vietnam and now the Middle-East. The repeated regurgitation is stressful, possibly a cause of fear, guilt or the acceptance you've alluded to."

"My point exactly. The truth about the Nazis, the holocaust and the horrors conducted by the KKK in the U.S. must be heard and remembered, but having them thrust upon us almost daily through the media structures traumatisms in the minds of many. I would even say that the matters shown or discussed are so tragic that it can become mind dulling, possibly to the point of building a kind of resistance to the horrors and a hardening of attitudes that may subsume the instinctual resistance to war that most of us embrace."

"I would add, Basil, that the age old argument about '*just war*' with all its pro and con opinions stifles the clearing of one's mind as to the rightness or wrongness of it."

"You're saying that the acceptance or expectation of war is internalized in some of us and replaces our natural objections to it."

"To some degree I do, Basil. The *just war* theorem; one that doesn't stop at the proposition that the best offense is a good defense, has been, and is promulgated as the *cantus firmus* of our existence. What I mean is that many of life's projections lead back to war and its implications. Is it any wonder that we are troubled by its constancy?"

"Historically I think Hitler's attempt to exterminate the Jews is perhaps the most relevant impact on the collective minds of all. I would assign its cause to the ancient hatred of Jews dating from the beginnings of Christianity."

"An extension of an age old hatred carried forth by despots."

"One might ask, '*Who killed the Jews?*'"

"Ask, and you'll find an astonishing absence of responsibility, neither Eichmann nor Speer, nor those who carried out the orders, so who killed the Jews? Were they human? The world is to this day revulsed and forever more will be."

"My point is that we are condemned to live with that knowledge of man's inhumanity to man."

"And so it goes, Basil. Genocide by an abattoir regime. Does it not, my friend? Where is the love?"

"Now this fine waterfront restaurant we choose for our night-out dinner is nearing time to close."

"Did you enjoy dinner, Suzanne?"

"Of course, Basil, but please, no more war talk. Can we cruise some on the Harley? Our dinner conversation was trying. We seem to be writing our book on the road. The dinner was elegant thank you. By the way, the next go-out dinner is on me."

"If you like we can swing on down-Cape. I've heard that the National Seashore in Eastham is nice and it's just down the road a bit"

"Yes. Let's do that. They say the National Seashore beach and walkways is a wonderful place, and it's a place we've never been."

They rolled on down the road, stopping near the park entrance in Eastham. Darkness revealed a delicious gentian-starry sky reaching to the horizon. They sensed their beings held within a glorious ethereal surround of timeless meditation. The evening progressed and later Suzanne looking at Basil's Harley noted it hadn't become a pumpkin. She squeezed Basil's hand an hour past midnight. They reluctantly mounted up to roar away biker style.

Suzanne and Basil arrived at their habitats an hour or so later. They stumbled through a courteous and embarrassingly self-conscious goodnight. Their hands reluctantly parted. A pre-breakfast swim on the high tide around seven was agreed. Suzanne's girlish intuition conveyed a wisdom of the ages: the writing of our book is primal.

⚊⊹ ⊹⚊

Basil hit the rolling surf with a chilling shriek as I watched from my kitchen window. It was seven; the circling seagulls squawked, demanding their morning repast. The morning was chilly. I surrendered the cottage warmth to toss chunks of bread skyward. We endured a brief swim, then raced back inside.

Later I served breakfast as Basil spoke, "Have you noticed we seem to do our best work while we're eating?"

"I think so too. We're food oriented writers. Maybe we should 'work-in' until *old sol* finds the beach.

"You know, I got to thinking last night how very much boredom influences out lives," declared Basil pouring half-in-half in his coffee.

"Well, that's really a fresh approach. One I've never heard. Is it me, Basil?" Suzanne shot back standing by the stove, hands on hips.

"Oh, Suzanne! On instant reflection I realize how foot-in-mouth that sounded. Shall I go to the *'what I meant part*?'"

"Yes, I think it best, Basil."

"Okay. It is said that boredom is the desire for desires. To me, it is the resultant frustration in the attempt to accomplish those desires that leads to boredom. We have desires, like things we would like to do, but the demands of our world, especially the workaday world, causes most of us to leave some on a back burner and sometimes never to pick up on them. You see? Nothing personal."

"You're certainly not talking about us. Got it!"

"Of course I'm not, Suzanne. This idea to write something together has captivated me."

"I want to expand a little on what you just said. The problem isn't necessarily the fault of the individual feeling that frustration either. I see two causes, one is the self imposed demand to adhere to the triviality of everydayness, sometimes by reason of financial exigency. The problem is that so many of us do so, without understanding that it doesn't have to control us. Like, let's leave room for life. The boredom you speak of can be overcome. Of course, a short answer is to get a life, get a job, or find something interesting to claim your time. You and I know that this advice isn't a final solution. Some of us find it necessary to work far below our talent and capability. Awareness of this is manifest within any person, like we know it, guy, most of us want the challenge the right job can bring," said Suzanne.

"Like wow! Repetitive tasks in the workplace or even in the home suggests to me a need to breakaway. Imagine what a lack of fulfillment one experiences when he or she must perform a periodic task without end."

"Do you think that repetition leads to the boredom that takes us down that black hole?" she asked.

"Definitely yes. Not only what we think of as ordinary life, the same things day and night, even things like being obsessed with soap operas or the evening news."

"Certainly boredom isn't confined to only the repetition of the workplace. What about '*I don't want to play this game anymore,*' rationale?"

"I've heard of what you speak. For sure though, uncountable numbers of that declaration has emanated from sheer boredom of whatever was in progress. And you know, the *game* could be an action or situation from digging clams to installing parts in a car factory, or any repetition our imaginations suggest."

"You are so funny, Basil. I hinted at some that relate to the marriage bed, but shall remain nameless. I would add that the experience of overwhelming dullness accompanied by an absence of intellectual stimulation will activate the feature we call boredom."

"I'll vote for intellectual stimulation always. Do you speak of a boring marriage bed from experience, Suzanne?"

"Now look! I never said that. I must have picked it up from some erotic romance novel."

"Now that we've so cleverly identified the causal meanings, what about how to deal with it? Can we eradicate it, exercise some mental gymnastics or something?"

"I can think of one action that could serve to overcome the strain of boredom in the workplace. I call it employing the *Zombie*. The ability exists within us to assign the performance of a repetitive or unbearable task to the *Zombie*. Its innate talent to complete the assignment is manifest within us. But wait, there's more!"

"Sounds like county fair hucksterism, Suzanne; 'But wait, there's more!'"

"Let me tell you why, Basil. Because this is a big load to absorb for some of us. Like perhaps you've experienced driving somewhere and not remembering a thing about the driving. Ever hear of that? Of course! You've mentioned it. You know why it occurred? It happened your mind had other things to ponder. Now we've reached that plateau where one readily understands that if one can drive a car from x to z, then why not let the friendly Zombie help you perform certain boring tasks?"

"I can't help but think that your approach is a saving one. Saving one from boredom that is. Does this apply to washing the dishes - stuff like that?"

"Why not? It could be in the restaurant where you clean dishes and place them on the rack in the dishwasher. Do you get my drift, Basil?"

"Yes. I think I've got it. I'm ready to expound on another solution to this boredom thing. If scrubbing dishes in the restaurant of your choice isn't intellectually stimulating enough I suggest you find an alternative, like another job, move on up to something of interest. I'm serious you know. Let it be known that you are seeking an alternative to your boredom."

"As long as you've gone this far, Basil, then I want to insert another means to avoid boredom. In a word; substitution. I'm speaking of that substitution either during the course of your activity or something that serves your creative interest during other times."

"Let's beware of too easy substitutions. Some call them hobbies."

"We've said a lot on how to overcome the boredom factor," Suzanne replied knowingly.

⟞⟡⟡⟝

"How about a picnic?" Suzanne shielded her eyes while absorbing the sun's assuring invitation to frolic with nature in some lush rendezvous.

"Let's go where we can prepare shrimp. I feel like smothering myself in hot sauce today," said Basil.

"I know of an idyllic spot where we can grill. It's a hilltop profusely grassy and with an easy footpath to the summit. We can be there in time for lunch."

"Sounds like the much sought path to the mountain top, Suzanne."

"That's close. It is a kind of small plateau. Before you tread the allegoric path would you please put the grille in the back of my Jeep?"

Our picturesque but uneventful drive passed in subjective talk about the ease of scripting our way through each stage of life. The past few days had activated a self awareness in us and now the question; simply if we're not what we think we are, raised a simple refutation stirring denial. We found our destination without any decision. Suzanne's description of the plateau was perfect. We followed the stone pathway to the top where a small natural flatland sustained a stand of tall pines shading several Adirondack chairs and some picnic tables.

Our charcoal briquettes glowed. Soon Suzanne called, Aussie style "Your '*shrimp is on the Barbie*' and then "Let's go on with our trip-talk. We were getting to a subject well known for its philosophic argumentation. You know, it's the self-doubt thing; the so called fallacy of insignificance."

"So, where's the beef, Suzanne?"

"First, I say we should realize that self doubt is commonplace within us. We should avoid and reject the negativity of perceived

51

limitations so common in our culture. I think all of us should question the trueness of remaining in any structured way, especially where conformity raises resistance causing pain. Am I here by choice? Our fit in the societal culture is often shaped by our desire to conform to the current environment and all of those influences marked by common acceptance within that stratum. If negativity is present a prudent departure may provide welcome relief. This should apply regardless of one's walk in life. Simply don't follow a script not meant for you. One should seek relief in another milieu and force the issue of change. Self awareness of your condition will prompt change."

"There you go again, using my word milieu. Like *'I'm outta here!,'* right Suzanne? I would add it helps to know that most human activity is purposeful. It's easy to adopt the attitude that you can raise the ceiling of your limitations. There's ecstasy in trying the new. Transcend to another experience and by the way, did I mention that you used that buzz word again; *milieu?*"

"Allow me to place some restraint on your uninhibited approach to life, Basil. Perhaps the most important of all; control the ego. We often expect the wrong things to give us happiness. Firstly, define happiness as you see it. Life everywhere is a condition in which much is endured but seemingly little meets our enthusiastic definition of happiness. Live with it. One of the best approaches is to eradicate from the mind those desires that are falsities and lead to futility. Gross materialism ranks high among them. If we purge those selfish desires, the practice of avarice, our approach to the wholeness of life opens to us, one in which we embrace a rational style of living without fear. Many things that previously snapped at our heels or bit us elsewhere are in absentia. The gods we might dethrone are the same as those idolized and given currency in our conscious world."

"I know of another area of interest we might explore, Suzanne. I call it life's long thoughts."

"Just what are these long thoughts, Basil? No, no, let me guess; are they the forever remembrances, those estuaries of retained thoughts lingering on and on?"

"Sort of. Don't you have a backup of things that are always there, thoughts that are only occasionally persistent, questions looking for answers? I mean things that seem to be imponderable, resisting quantification."

"I'm turning my recorder on, Basil. I can't keep all this in my head."

"How have you been doing it?"

"My recall is pretty good. Nights I enter everything on my laptop, at least whatever I remember. So, anyhow, you name one of your imponderables and then I'll name one and we can see who runs out first."

"O.K., Suzanne. Here's one for the recorder; Do you sometimes feel that you're losing touch with your aboriginal self? I'm living in a culture that may or may not have any attachment whatsoever with my origins. Am I miscast? I know I wasn't hatched on a rock - my senses sometimes urge me to return to some cultural ambiguity of the past. I seem to have a latent desire to return, but to what? What social structures are right for me? And I use the word ambiguity advisedly. After all, how many of us know that much about our origins. Should they be a matter of interest? How much do other people care - I mean about themselves?"

"I think we could write a whole book confined to the questions you ask, Basil. I will take the last question first; to my own experience with friends and others, I'd say that people are interested a lot in their origins. Some of us have a long line of ancestors who for whatever reason maintained a sort of dialogue with successive generations. Their wonderment must be somewhat satisfied as to who, what and where. Surely those who have come to this country forcibly have a story to tell, like my forebears. Those of us who have limited knowledge of ancestry are traveling without papers so to speak, like me, and knowing only that their relations came from such and such a nation or place is lean indeed."

"What we seem to be saying is that widely different perceived needs of one's aboriginal past is where the interest turns. If you want to know, go fishing."

"I will ask you one thing, Basil. how certain is anyone of the actions of one's ancestors? Perhaps it's better not to know."

"I've read that some decline the new fashion of DNA based genealogy, and by the way, your affinity for the sand dunes, Suzanne. How would you define such an unusual feeling of belonging?"

"You really want to know? I mean, I have my unpleasant story to tell. I want to tell it. You may as well know. Like I said, my mom never married. I guess she was seeking perfection because she told me my father's contribution came from a sperm bank. She lied to me Basil. Just why she never said and I never believed her anyhow. When you speak of our aboriginal selves and ancestry one could say I'm sans-dad."

"Stop, stop, stop! Don't put yourself through this. I don't need to know, really, Suzanne. I can accept what you've told me. Don't feel guilt over it."

"You did ask Basil. The dunes influence? Not a clue. Anyway, the worst is out. I need to tell you; I've been a loner too long and I've been closer to you than anyone for a long long time. You deserve to know. Here's my dune story: It was my first morning here, a Saturday, when I decided to walk the beach. I had no idea that the dunes would capture me. It was early. I was chilly and barefoot. The tide was filling the ruts in those sandy ripples. When I got to the dunes their dark shadows almost reached the water's edge. The herring gulls were everywhere sounding their incessant calls. They ignored my attention as they scurried along selecting edible bits deposited by the tide. I zipped my jacket. The dune's dark and windless silence spoke of death. I stood facing the enormity of the impenetrable dunes on that sandy substrate and sensed a never before loneliness. A damp haze obscured the sun. For a second I thought I glimpsed a figure walking in that gray surround."

"You've mesmerized my curiosity, Suzanne, but do you really want to go on?"

"Yes. I felt no fear for a moment, but then I ran and backed against the vertical wall of one dune facing the sea. Suddenly I re-called the memory of one day I was lost in a haunting wood. Those memories seemed to press me against that dark mass. I must have fainted. I awoke to the incoming tide splashing over me. I ran cra-zily back to my cottage and crashed on the bed crying, where I slept until dark."

Basil moved to hold her.

"Please hold me for a while until I stop shaking," Suzanne cried.

"I will. I will," said Basil, fighting emotion.

Suzanne wondered, 'Has my story destroyed our budding friend-ship? There we were horizontal on the grass that afternoon until the charcoal embers went gray. I felt good with Basil's arm around me. He kissed my cheek, thinking I was sleeping. When I awoke the sun was in the west. We relaxed, hand in hand, looking straight up at the sky.

Suzanne spoke, "This is such a nice way to end the day, Basil. I'm glad we came to this idyllic spot."

Basil was enraptured, he mumbled, "Me too." and pausing said, "Please, let's just rest here a while."

A moment later he said, "You know what? A lot of us don't know who our daddy is! And I have a *yes-but;* My heart goes out to you, but Suzanne, the depth of our relationship became evident with your story."

"Oh dear Basil, I thought you would ride off on your motor-cycle and forget we ever met. Now you know. I have a memory of the dunes and I don't know whether it actually happened or I imagined it. I can't believe what I told you really happened, you know, it happened but it didn't. It reminds me of something about dreams, something René Descartes said; *'Painters when they study to create satyrs, however strange, can only rarely give them forms fictitious and absolutely false.'* Maybe I was lost in sleep and astonishment like Descartes."

"What I'm getting to is this, Suzanne. After your disclosure of that great fright the impenetrable shell you lived in cracked. What I'm saying is that your moment of declaration brought us closer."

"Are you getting to the soul thing? Like, now we've found our inner child?"

"I don't know, really I haven't the foggiest. Let me ask you; the other day when we first visited the dunes in Barnstable, you told me your attraction was in their isolation, the silence and some forbidding secrets they might hold. My question is why?"

"I am fascinated by them, Basil. I think for me they're like what the sea and the mountains are for others. I deliberately withheld today's confession. Wouldn't you? Maybe I'm obsessing how the dunes draw me to them. I'm sorry. Won't you forgive me?"

"My dear Suzanne; I'm not thinking in conditional terms. You never have to ask me for forgiveness."

Basil rolled to face me. I responded. We embraced. Our hugs lead to kissing without restraint, a timeless ecstasy.

Basil spoke as he drove back to the cottages, "I thought of something, Suzanne. If we think in terms of your teleological strengths which relate to the study of ultimate causes in nature or of actions in relation to their ends or utility we might discover what this is all about."

Suzanne heard a voice from far away. She slept. Basil sat up straight and stretched, thinking; *'Had enough chit-chat for the afternoon. I guess it can wait.'*

They rolled into the cottage compound at dusk. Suzanne, awake from her nap, spoke, "I'll make dinner. I need an hour or so. Come over whenever, Basil."

⫘⫘

Dinner began quietly. Basil offered a brief prayer of thanks for the sustenance.

She asked casually across the narrow kitchen table, "You do believe then, don't you?" the question nearly obscured her intent to find the truth.

Basil felt the sting, "Yes I do, but don't get religion-specific for I might disappoint you."

"You just ducked around me and left a huge question mark. You know that?"

"You want to get into this tonight? I'll talk, but I think you'll catch my drift. I'm just not that devout a Christian, although I'm not attached to any other belief."

"I would like to hear your definition of a Christian. And yet, I can't picture you as a religious whacko either. Can I put that on the table?"

"Why not? I've been called a bunch of things, but not that, at least not recently."

"Go ahead Basil, I've had my nappy time so I think I can stay awake if you want to expound on where you are in this wonderful screwed-up world."

"The time is ripe. It surely will be no more strange than your dune hopping. So okay, turn on your recorder."

"Run, Basil, run!"

"First off, like I said, I'm not going to get religion specific, neither will I speak of each entity, nor denominationally; my reason being that it isn't germane to my story. Recall, I mentioned how my youthful breaking away from some traditions occurred, I tired of a lifestyle predicated on what others thought appropriate for me. I was nicely told how to live, what to uphold, like I said an existence in lockstep within a surround of nanny-like rules. Even told what to buy. Like I said before, I did accept those rules back then with all the thoughts, moralities, and religious teachings and writings, both new and from the ages. Then, and increasing more so with time, I recognized the power of repressive propriety and how very extreme the power of authority really is. The fact was, Suzanne, like millions of us, my mind was made up for me by well meaning people with an agenda. But, those very things energized me for change."

"Maybe you were luckier than some of us. You heard the status-quo train conductor yell: *'all aboard!'* Aha, but destination not! You tore up your ticket. You knew at an early age it wasn't for you and lucky for you no one beat you with a stick to fixate your brain," Suzanne smiled with admiration as she poured our first wine of the evening.

"I want to tell you what I think. A lot of us are staring into a can of worms because we are attempting to worship and live our lives in accordance with a religion contrived by others."

"That's a strong word; *contrived.*"

"I'm suggesting an upgrading and here's why: we're ruled by tradition, compelled to accept and perform in imitation, told to try to live like Jesus and forced to repetitive habits initiated during ancient times."

"I never heard of this kind of talk before!"

"You may not ever again either."

"Are you suggesting we scrap the system?"

"Of course not. What I'm saying is that the traditions live on as a subjective thing being hammered on constantly by self appointed authority who compel us to accept their various and sometimes absurd interpretations."

"There's a thing called the second coming that assures us we shall be totally enlightened."

"You bring up my next point. We need the initial actions brought to the forefront to enable the world's people to freely internalize God's logic and meaning. To me this has been notably absent from the teachings so rigorously adhered to."

"This isn't what I thought you were going to say, Basil."

"Now, may I lay out my rationale? I have a word for it; it's called syncretism. I initiated this before I'd heard of the word. My effort was an attempt to unite and harmonize without applying a really critical examination or looking for logical unity. I wanted to reconcile contrary beliefs and I deliberately did what you might call mix and match. It became complicated and some things didn't meld, but I merged what I could and analogized several discrete traditions in theology. The upshot of this was I found a unity allowing an inclusive approach to many faiths. You're the philosophy major, Suzanne, so you will recall something attributed to Georg Hegel; '*In theology it's not so much the creed of the church that passes for Christianity, as that everyone to a greater or less degree makes a Christianity of his own to tally with his convictions.*'"

"I was ready to exclaim '*holy cow*', before it became so inappropriate," replied Suzanne, adding, "You seem to be saying that God was revealed in many ways. Tell me, what really got you started on this track of the infidel?"

"May I remind you of my prayer of supplication, giving thanks for our repast? This is not the voice of infidelity! No disbelief here."

"Let me understand; you do but you don't, right? It's like me, you know, I had the horrid recall at the dunes, but then I didn't."

"Before you suggest that I apply for admission to join the satyrs of your acquaintance, let me explain," Basil retorted, placing his hands palms down on the dinner table.

"Please do, Basil," replied Suzanne striking a look of negative deference.

"Even near my beginnings I felt like a caged member of the *chicken-coop society*. The prevalent attitude of the cultural pattern of belief didn't fit. Many agree that we live in a religion obsessed country. My contrary attitude was because I tired quickly of the prevailing mythos; I tired of accepting the stylized exhortations. That's how I got on this path."

Suzanna spoke; "Lots of people have made major changes, both in their beliefs and of course where they worship. You didn't find satisfaction, Basil. You are a bit of maverick you know."

"Let me tell you what I'm not. I'm not out to destroy organized religion nor to replace it with superstitions. Those who would do that are the maggots tearing at Christianity's vitals."

Then came Suzanne's stinger! "It seems to me you're an apostate, in that you have renounced your religious faith or have simply abandoned a previous loyalty," her Cheshire grin levitated between them.

Basil's reply was defensive, "Suzanne, you pushed my buttons with that one. Will you allow me to dig my way out of this inexorable pit?"

"But of course, Basil," the Cheshire grinned in.

"Let me say this, the heretic might get thrown out, but probably wants to belong, and indeed, often claims to represent the authentic expression of the faith. An apostate, by contrast, rejects the faith and religious community altogether. I'm going to put my reply within the context of only myself because I don't fit the description of a true apostate. There is little if any distinction in this country of insiders and outsiders, that to me is a necessary to enforce the definition of apostate. Our spiritual questing is relatively promiscuous in that so many of us are never exclusively in one religion very long and find ourselves elsewhere for devotions on another day. Continuity? Not! To leave certain religions is to apostatize, while to leave a myriad of others, notably mainline Christian groups, is simply to float from one to another. Aren't we tilling new soil here? Float is such a cavalier term to me. I would think that those making change in their religion or Deity would find a less jaunty word. You may have read that a Phrygian named Quintus, is said to have abandoned his salvation when presented with the choice of renouncing Christ or being killed by wild beasts in the arena. The Emperor Julian, abandoned his Christian commitments and embraced pagan philosophy around the fourth century as some people recognized the incompatibility of Jesus and Helios, the Sun God. I never thought there should be social consequences for leaving the faith. I appreciate that my church makes room for patchwork, for doubt, for moving in and out repeatedly.

I've thought, thanks to this freedom, I have attained a more comprehensive understanding of these matters than I could have otherwise."

Suzanne looked pensive, "You've made your case. Just consider the extremism when a more recent notable, the writer, Salmon Rushdie, was issued a fatwa calling for his assassination in 1989 when his satirical novel, *The Satanic Verses* was declared *anti-Islam* by Iran's Ayatollah Ruhollah Khomeini."

"You bring me to my critical point, Suzanne; If anyone is swimming in an element they wish to abandon, tolerating a painful or a stultifying ethos, get rid of the god or whatever it is. Free yourself of the repetition of certain acts you find dull and boring. Eliminate them to attain a balanced and rational life."

"You did that!" she replied.

"I did. One thing I've avoided is what I call '*death of the intellect.*' My hunch is that anything forced upon us in the areas of political, ethical, social, aesthetics, and the religious dulls one's senses to some extent. Insofar as these are backed up time after time, the mind internalizes them and ceases to actively pursue other avenues. The mind must be open to a rational understanding to maintain a fair balance."

"So! Oh great guru, just where is that fair balance of yours?"

"The circumstances of my life like I just related caused me to seek an alternative to my past experience. You ask of fair balance? My reply is there is none. Go back to our quick conversation at the coffee shop."

"Can't forget. I said your bike was classy and you almost exploded. I'm sleepy. The day is catching up again my friend. It's time to say nighty-nite!"

Basil got up reluctantly as he recalled their tenderness that afternoon. He wanted so much to hold her again. He held out his hand. She came to him.

He wrapped his arms around her, "May I kiss you goodnight?"

"Yes Basil. And then be a good boy and run along."

"In the morning then. Bye."

"Good night, Basil."

———

"What'll be today, Suzanne? Sightseeing? The beach, Shoppe hopping?" A flock of winged guests obliterated his voice. She beckoned him closer.

"I was thinking, would you like to pack a lunch and go to the beach on the south side, maybe down Cape, towards Provincetown?"

"Looks like a good beach day. I think we should get a few more licks in on our book."

"Tell you what, Basil, we could rent a cabana so we don't get too much sun. We can pick up a seafood lunch along the way and stay as long as we want."

As they carried their stuff over the boardwalks their appetites struck. Another sunny beach day and tide just right for a swim, and then to eat and to work. Basil had finished his lunch when he thought he must introduce an idea worthy for the book. He had hesitated to get so involved that day, but knew that Suzanne's intent was to work.

Basil spoke, "I have a thought to submit."

"I was thinking the same thing! Ever since yesterday crazy bells have been going off with the most provoking idea," Suzanne replied excitedly.

"Well, then you go ahead. I can tell you're burning with desire to tell me."

"I'll begin and you chime in whenever. Now here goes; understand, this is beyond most anyone's realm of reality, but since my experience on the morning I told you about I got scared. I figure I should face my goblins."

"Are you thinking what I think? Are you conjuring up some way to describe our very beings? Do you think that big pile of sand is going to tell you the great secrets, where all those thinkers of the world have failed," Basil wagged his head solemnly.

"That's not it at all, Basil! I'm thinking we can envision how we perceive ourselves, lifting some shadowy veils and gain some transparency. My idea has merit, does it not?"

"Suzanne, come on, maybe we've been out in the sun too long. I have a question. Do you really think the dunes have some mystical power?"

"After what I felt that morning, yup, I'll confirm that."

"What if your experience was something totally imaginary, like you were suffering from some illness or hadn't eaten breakfast? Maybe you hallucinated."

"Oh Basil, you don't know and neither do I! Would you go there with me some morning?"

"Tomorrow. We'll go tomorrow," Basil declared with finality.

Suzanne added, "I'm not saying we should attempt to seek the counsel of the dead. What do you think, should we really try this?"

"Yes, yes, tomorrow; we'll go tomorrow. I hope the dead remain enjoying their eternal bliss and reject the evil disturbance as the actions of two idiotic earthlings."

"Now you're making fun," she remarked.

Dusk was fast approaching. They prepared to return to the cottages. After a final swim Basil bought some cold drinks from a nearby *roach-coach.* and they departed.

⊷╫╫⊶

Suzanne prepared an early dinner. Sitting at her small dining table she said, "You mentioned a thought. Want to let me hear it now."

"By now I've modified it. I'm thinking that people know what it is our society requires as essentials for life.

"I like that, Basil, except if everyone knows then why bother to say it? Would some people find that offensive?"

"It isn't that this hasn't been said in the past. What would this person or that person say is certainly justifiable if the reasoning adheres to the individuals known principles. Think of the many who form associations dedicated to the thought and beliefs of others both living and dead."

"Some times, Basil, your stream of consciousness is confusing. I said before, truth is rather conditional. Like truth of a belief should be thought of within the consistency of other beliefs. Don't you think?

"Alright Ms. Philosophy. I think I got it. I want to think in terms of the demands we make of ourselves and others to establish our perceived essentials in life."

Suzanne replied, "Perhaps you could do that during our visitation to the dunes, like confirm my anxiety."

"Yes, I promised tomorrow. You said anxiety, Suzanne; are you sure you don't mean fear?"

"I interpret anxiety as like when you take a walk in the woods and you hope you don't encounter a bear. Now fear, well, that's when the bear taps you on the shoulder. I sense a certain reluctance in your response and I've thought it over and now I think whatever my goblins are they were only in my imagination. Nothing meaningful at all."

"Let's hold that thought. What do you say we walk to that frightful spot of yours to satisfy us once and for all?"

"Tomorrow."

"Yup, tomorrow."

⚓

That day broke with fog and heavy clouds. Suzanne commented, "It was just like this."

"What was?"

"The weather."

"I'll get something going on the grill," said Basil as he waited for the charcoal to glow and waved off an occasional swooping gull. Suzanne walked across the deck armed with stale bread to capture the birds' attention.

"Bacon and eggs ready in a few minutes, Suzanne. You want'em over-easy like before?"

"Yes. Morning again sweetheart." She stood on her toes to kiss him, whispering, "Here's some coffee. Now don't burn the biscuits!"

"I remember from my history class. Do you recall who burned the biscuits?"

"Yes I do. Everybody knows that. Let's get on with it, Basil. I feel like shooing my scary-cats away."

"You're singing a different tune now, babe. Sounds like the macabre spooks are done for," quipped Basil shooting a quizzical look at Suzanne.

"Let's go soon. I want the sun and the fog just like it is right now."

"I'm almost ready. You said about twenty minutes to reach he dune?"

"About. Let's hold hands as we walk."

As they walked, tracing the uneven tidal swirls, Basil said, "This eerie misty dimness imparts an aura of intrigue."

"How very theatric. I should write that one down," she reproached gently and squeezed his hand.

"I see the gray beast now. You're scared ain't ya!"

"Now walk slowly. We'll approach the dunes exactly as best as I can recall. This way any evil presence will have every opportunity to harass us. Gosh, Basil, this morning is so like that first day. Come this way. Follow me and stand right over this way. See anything?"

"Not yet. Should I whistle or somethin?"

"Come over here with me and lean against this monstrous dune wall."

⇥⊩ ⊩⇤

"Anything yet?" quipped Basil, his patience provoked by the penetrating chill, "I'm not intimidated by this gray pile of sand. Let's shove off for reality."

"I was dreaming just now. We were in a bright faraway forest surrounded by an incredible primeval darkness. We were standing together holding hands. There were songbirds and a fox."

"How about it, Suzanne. You wanna stay in your forest primeval or what?"

"Stay, I want to stay. I sense something cold and evil and yet I'm warm and happy."

"Maybe you're freezing to death. I know I am. Ready to go?"

"Stay Basil. Relax and let's drift for a while."

"I'm on a short leash. I'll stay, but babe, I was thinking. Maybe your enthusiasm to delve into the nature of this dune is a little too close to the bone. Who knows, some intermingling or diffusion might easily occur if we're casual."

"You're suggesting we get casual with a sand dune? Now who's the looney? And what is this diffusion you speak of?"

"Know what? I'm scared. When I first arrived on the Cape I thought I was fairly rational. Now I don't know. Diffusion is like an intermingling of substances, some kind of oneness in a medium."

"Maybe I'm the crazy, Basil, but I'm standing in the diffusion. You sound strange. I sense that your *casual dune* prompts you to get on with it. What do you want to do?"

"We could stay in this mysterious consciousness or maybe invoke the dune's diffusion another time."

"You know what, Basil, this can't be in our time element; it may be instantaneous. I'm feeling strange for I have no concept of time."

"Mine is an opaque nothingness. You've reached a further depth than I. Besides, I only wanted to be a passenger on this ethereal train ride anyhow."

"Listen to me! I'm standing in that sunny forest again. It's beautiful."

"My imagination doesn't match yours. I feel a sort of deep meditation and a quantum lateral exchange of thoughts."

"We asked and now we must endure the consequences. Do you feel privileged we may have escaped ourselves?"

"Give me a minute to think. I'll say yes. It's beyond insightful isn't it."

"Wouldn't it be great to gain wisdom from those iconic people we've studied; the philosophers, theologians, poets, writers, and academia's masters?"

"It ain't gonna happen here, Suzanne. You said your sunny forest is enclosed in evil and darkness. That's more akin to Solzhenitsyn's Gulag, or some atavistic renewal of autos-da-fe revulsion. I'd call this a temporal recourse to the Chekhovian stage; that's my take of what happened on this timeless trip."

"Our tête-à-tête is wrong place, wrong time!"

"I felt like a klutz when we walked here today. Now I sense a kind of catharsis, like I've purged some fault," Basil confessed.

"I'm awake and now I feel fully conscious, but what have I done?" Suzanne asked.

"Here, I want to give you this. I wrote this last night after thinking about what you said. May I read it?"

"Of course, I'd love to hear it.

"Ready? Here goes:"

Mysticism

I walked the sandy dunes one day
Seeking a likely place to pray.
I lingered, fearful of Plato's
Dark Cave of Illusion,
But found no such element existed here.
Instead my Spiritual transcendence
Courtesy of Meister Eckhart's Mystic Path
Showed clearly that God exists,
Answering the age old skepticism
For God and I were momentarily One.

"Oh my, Basil! That is beautiful. How did you ever think of it?"

"Like I told you before, I have a bunch of books in my biker-bag. One of them speaks of Mysticism, so I read up on it. Then I wrote it for you."

"You're a dear. Our trial and error approach wasn't a winner, but I thank you. Why isn't Mysticism more highly regarded by Christians?"

"It is highly regarded among some. My guess is that the mystic experience is so rare. I think Mysticism belongs as a complementary relationship with religions; however a strenuous gap exists particularly one of a lack of correlation in Christianity. Skepticism by some authorities is also a wedge expelling a more universal acceptance of Mysticism. A factor influencing this thought is that those who experience Mysticism often have values and beliefs contrary to Christianity, so some authorities question the validity of it in the entirety," Basil said.

"That kind of talk seems like a giant step from your mathematics and political science specialties to me."

"Well, yeah, somewhat. My thought is that everything is interconnected in some manner like the idea that we're all one. It's not me, babe; some great minds have said so."

"How so, Basil?"

"Well, Leopold Kronecker, a 19th century mathematician said: *'God created the integers.'* I think Stephen Hawking concurs because his name is on the cover of the book of the same name."

"The integers work don't they?"

"You betcha. For me, absolutely. But you know there does exist a kind of parting of the ways in the use of signs and symbols in their interpretation and use in Christianity and mathematics."

"Oh Mr. Absolutely! You're going to tell me aren't you?" Suzanne couldn't hide her amusement.

"I'm glad you asked, but of course," he replied, catching her absurdity.

"C'mon Basil, let's wander back to the cottages while you tell me."

"Well, mathematicians have used signs from the git-go like plus and minus, an x or a dot or brackets for an equation, also the sign for division, but then they needed more. So they borrowed from the Greek alphabet like for summation and others, thereby mixing signs and symbols to indicate math operations."

"May I interrupt? I've read of this. You're about to tell me about Dr. Paul Tillich's statements on religious language. How the symbol participates in meaning and power which is not itself and that the use of a sign is non-participatory in that it points as an indicator to such as a traffic signal."

"Yes. We came to it from two directions. He explained the confusion of language when the mathematician undertook to apply symbols as signs."

"Basil. Isn't it interesting how such a distraction can exist?

"Right on! Distractions indeed. I've read of Emerson's defining the use of symbols in *The Poet*. Symbols are also employed to obtain compensatory substitutes, to unleash suppressed desires, pride of ownership, to impress another person. Proposals exploit the underlying reasons to obtain the desired results. He said: '*We are far from having exhausted the significance of the few symbols we use.*'"

"And you will straighten this all out, right?"

"Afraid not. These varying interpretations are engrained. I don't conceive of any change. Hey Suzanne, I don't feel rushed either. No monkey on my back."

"Not even the one who stole your sunglasses and ran away?"

"Not even him."

"I sense the aura. There must be some kind of a force emitted by the dunes."

"Be humble now, Suzanne, don't try the water thing! Here, take my hand."

"Maybe we've juggled our neurons."

"Oh, come on. Now you're funning me. Besides, you're the one sensing that Mysticism in the dunes."

"Like you didn't? We're back. Come on in. I'll make coffee. Did you notice how our search for meaning seemed timeless?"

"Just now, yeah. For a while I thought we had received a cosmic download."

"I don't know, it was surely faster than my laptop. Do you remember like a dream; meeting some goddess of wisdom?"

"Nope. I'd have remembered a goddess. Nothing marvelous like that."

"You said you had some idea for our book. Time to share?"

"Of course, but first, I'm anxious about this entire thing. I read once of something Abraham Maslow mentioned in his book; *The Farther Reaches of Human Nature*, that was the enormous task between inspiration and the final product. The hard work, discipline, and the tossed early drafts."

"There you go again. Tell you what, I'll exert the discipline of a Marine Drill Sergeant! You work hard and stay on target."

"Yes mam! Message received. Let me get back on course; I think it's appropriate - let's see what you think. Maybe our morning's escapade activated my thoughts; My key word is *vanity*."

"Vanity. I recall it in Ecclesiastes. I'll turn the recorder on while you expound."

"You know how its been said: *All is vanity*?"

"Yes, but we know religion is a serious state of mind and the claim that *All is vanity* is the word of a dissipated skeptic. It is the dark corner of refutation in the absence of proof. One should beware the temptation of easy solutions."

"Would you believe a lot of stuff is vanity? I'm speaking of mans' vanity; it all comes down to pride, especially excessive pride. My interpretation of it connects vanity with class, and as you know, class is my current buzzword!"

"You don't think the big dune you snuggled up with transferred any wisdom to Mr. Basil, do you?"

"Na, no way. What I'm saying is, people seem to embrace a need for some sort of essential identify, a distinction, especially to emphasize a superiority or proudly display some glaringly self-produced characteristics.

"It took the magic dune to tell you? I knocked the slats off my crib when I first realized that! Hobbes called it vanity. Rousseau called it amour propre.

"I guess it didn't, but my interest brought me to see a complexity of our personal characteristics which I've packaged all inclusively as *class.* They are so closely interrelated in the ways we describe ourselves that I'll stand on my assumption that as an aggregate those many separables combine as *class.*

"Your assertion does establish class as a noun like the dictionary says."

"But Suzanne, observe that it applies to so many recognizable defining features, like gender, race, sexuality, nationality, religion, income, political orientation. Even those unfortunates said to be classless."

"I suppose its does. And who shall cast the first stone?"

"I get it. You know better than I that the Christian religion reveals that all men are brothers and it seeks to invalidate the accidents of history that divide the human race and has encouraged transcendence of race and class. And you know us to be a social failure; practicing racism, prejudice, and in the dark corners of our being a refusal to mingle with those 'others'. What of the *just world theory*, embraced by and perceived as *class - success to be* self confirmed. This is categorically reversed by those said to be *lower class* as not deserving of success, their disposition to success, those inborn traits, and lack of ability are noted, thereby building a defensive wall, like barricades to transparency, to comfort that self appointed superior class. Conversely, those who append the inferiority of lower class status to self justify their position in life more to circumstances such as prejudice, health, and environmental reasons. A blindness occurs in one's reality, the ego driven success person enjoys the comfort of personal experience. The poor and underprivileged face external limitations of decreased opportunity. They acknowledge their lower class status is chained to repetitious, boring, unwanted jobs as economics demand. In the minds of many it seems normal to reject the thought that bad things happen to good people. This is a form of escapism. We use defense mechanisms, myth dependent thinking like God's will, Karma, magic and all the while seeking to blame the unfortunate victims."

"Something of a tall order is missing from humanity's vision."

"Oh yeah. One might say it's a missing link."

"You're not going to tell me about the apes are you?"

"I never thought the apes were responsible for man's inconsistencies. I'm thinking of something ethereal."

"That may be the key," Suzanne replied.

"It doesn't leave much to work with, does it?"

"Basil! We're horsing around without coming right out with it! Much of humanity has lost the vision of God."

"I've obscured my point although that's what I'm getting to."

"Know what, Basil? I've been shoveling sand against the tide on this subject almost from the day we met and finally you crawl out from your shell of obscurity."

"The pendulum swings babe and this Boston dude has much to learn from the lovely Chicagoan called Suzanne," Basil cringed, knowing he's opened a can of worms.

⇥ ⇤

Suzanne directed her attention to a repetitious needling within. It suggested that her writing was mal-directed and lacking in the desired content. This combined with a reminder that she was a member of the age group called Millennials and the perpetuated charge describing them as having an irreparable penchant for demanding entitlements not prevalent in earlier generations. This aroused in her an uncommon anger and denial.

"We need to talk, Basil!" Suzanne's early a.m. announcement shook Basil's conscience, building an undeserved feeling of guilt.

"Your opening gambit usually precedes the end of a love affair, sweetheart. What is it?"

"I'm sorry Basil. I got kind of upset this morning about the guilt trip being hung on our generation, this severe critique of us Millennials."

"You mean like our desire for a better life, our love of materialism and stuff, a narcissism leading to non-work and that innate love of freedom?"

"That sounds pretty close to how we're defined."

"I'll plead guilty to most of it. I ask you; haven't earlier generations wanted to have a better life? Tell me it isn't so!"

"So, do you think our taking vacations is their reference?" She asked.

"Neither of us have made vacations habitual. We've both waited to finish our university education and now I think we deserve it. And, another thing, we're working every day on our book. And you're gainfully employed at the Coffee Shop."

"You're providing some relief, thank you. Here's another one, Basil. I think our book has too much pain from the past."

"May I kindly remind you, Suzanne, you said that the ancients, the philosophers and others of wisdom were great to draw upon while seeking answers."

"I know, I know. Well, I'm going to hold to that idea, but we need to build in a positive way. Otherwise our writing will be little more than a rerun of historical fact."

"Let's pitch it and find a new beginning."

"No. I can't agree with that. I want to grow on it, like keep on moving."

"What you're saying is that the wisdom of the past has merit."

"Just watch me, Basil. For one thing, the core of our being is built on the evolution of man. Our thinking is predicated on the trial and error of the past. Our fundamentals were recognized by the philosophers and prophets over the years."

"Sounds to me that a newborn has a kind of one-up by the way of inherited predispositions. Is this why man has built such a glorious world of peace and wonder?"

"Your fatuity is noted. Perhaps you should consider the fact of just who initiated the wars, the bigotry and those other actions that led man to where he is."

"You're getting around to my alter-argument; let me explain, is it not likely that a lack of evolutionary discipline in some who failed to develop the quality of restraint and a common morality, never reached that higher plateau, instead they live within a core-self of impulsive violence?"

"I question ourselves, Basil. You speak of the core-selves. Then what is your opinion of this? Are you and I rooted sufficiently within the realm of the intellect and do we have the depth to consider actually writing a book that has the faintest likelihood of helping anyone?"

"Only by reason of our collective motivation. Without it, I would ask God to be sure we tend to our fishing and make talk of cabbages and kings."

"Gosh Basil, you've never mentioned God in such serious ways. You're invoking God's grace by asking for the green light?"

"You know what, Suzanne, I'm overwhelmed that we're seriously planning to do this. It draws me to my very depths. I'm certain it challenges my being."

"Well, I never!" exclaimed Suzanne, adding, "Basil, you're right, this may be the time to pray."

⊨⊩ ⊪⊨

There's a new day a dawning, Basil. Make no mistake about it. Our decision yesterday is front burner today."

"I'm ready, Miss Suzanne! I thought about this last night, and know what?"

"Well, what?"

"How about we start at today's dilemma and work backwards?"

"Would you care to remove the mystique, Basil, for I'm quite ready."

"You know what it is, don't you? It's a creeping and somewhat prevailing attitude that mans progress is a causation encouraging a propensity within our collective culture to move from our established habit of church attendance to one of neglect. An increasingly number of those whose chief interests are societal problems have declared that religion is more of a hindrance than a help."

"You're saying that in the most church-going country perhaps in the world that people are neglecting the beliefs of our forefathers? Preposterous, Basil! This goes against everything sensible or reasonable."

"Au contraire, Suzanne! It's a trend within our culture. Not only here, but in other nations."

"So, what is this *causation*, to use your fancy word?"

"I have a hunch of what it is. In a word, it's a loss of faith, with its cause in the excesses of the church, both historical and current, the suggestion by some who are motivated more by the profit motive than their beliefs to follow or join in some whacked-out religious practice."

"Are you saying that the conventional Christian beliefs in common practice express the limits of credibility in many of us?"

"Yes. It's apparent that we believe in the existence of things that many of our contemporaries are unwilling to accept."

"Not only that, but people on either side of the argument are constantly exposed to the intriguing machinations and occasional nefarious schemes by those having various designs for any gullible believer."

"So, what is the upshot of all this? How does it affect the traditional Christian church?" she asked.

"It's the *boggle factor.* I call it the elasticity of faith. Some of us are extremely flexile and may bend one of two ways; either to reject anything seemingly non-sensible or the opposite by allowing it within one's realm of probability and valid belief."

"And what about the others, great guru?"

"Therein is a consistency of those who are deeply boggled by these extraneous inputs outside of the believers' tradition. Where one's judgments are predicated on the existence of certainties, a complication of understanding accompanied by a failure of one's own continuum becomes hazardous to the churches' membership roles."

"But many of us accept or reject certain things proclaimed by other Christians to be true. One that comes to mind is the power of petitionary prayer," said Suzanne.

"Yes indeed, and you are the chosen one to enlighten me on that very subject."

"I'm not that sure, Basil, but I do have some thoughts. One thing I think is appropriate today is that one should not exclude the intellect from participating in anything we do and this must include our belief systems."

"What of those quasi but sensible beliefs that form the feelings of a believer's faith?

"Religion is the feeling and experience we hold as divine. To devalue these in moments of doubt, a kind of alternate I don't deny. A sort of controlling balance seems to drive us within the spiritual and material desires, a sort of passion for both."

"It's inconstant then. You run strong or not depending on some factors within your being or nature."

"Yes, Basil, kai su Brutus?"

"You know I'm not criticizing, Suzanne, only surprised at the declaration. If I've accomplished one thing in life, it's that I feel I'm a man among men."

"How so, Basil?"

"It's a consciousness, a demand for truth, for one to confess his fallibility and humanness and to toss his pride."

"It must surely be a work in progress," Suzanne remarked, her Cheshire grin aflame.

"Excuse me, for I haven't your psychological advantage. I want to be the man who influences others. One size fits all the minds of men, not! The bed of Procrustes, that cutting off legs or stretching the body to obtain a force fit no, no, not our minds."

"I was thinking while you slipped between Procrustes' sheets how very right you are. The minds of man are not in accord and I'll venture the variations in religious belief systems serve as an example."

"Perhaps I'm the unwitting victim of a lack of religious inculcation. I told you how I minced around trying this church and that church. I became anxious over the ongoing arguments of creedal beliefs."

"What did you find?"

"I found that many of our own find some religious convictions to be important to their lives even if not founded on reason and that so many denominations and even non-denominationals declare their approach to religion to stand uniquely alone."

"And speaking as of today, what does your mind say?"

"That these variations are nothing more or less than beliefs evolved over time as men choose them. I settled on God as a loving God and to otherwise know God to me is futile."

"Do you feel a loss because of your self imposed separation?" she asked.

"No. But I came to the realization that man is a herd animal and is healthy when he lives as a social being, but as I've said, I no longer subscribe to any denomination."

"But you are a believer!"

"Yes. Like Aristotle declared that man seeks knowledge, man also seeks his own truth. I've had the pleasure to seek it out."

"You'll find, Basil, we're not alone in that admission. I've awakened to the knowledge of my being. My religious reality came from a self divided. I was consciously wrong, feeling inferior and unhappy. Things change. The way our beliefs work for us is the final test. I've found a kind of insight, one that calls to my attention the fact that I'm too often preoccupied with myself. Religious insight makes men conscious of the sinfulness of their preoccupation with self. The devout must disassociate selfish desire from the will-to-live. There are limitations in religion that do encourage that one purifies their life like family rather than the problems of complex political relations or the like. A fortunate insight causes men to be conscious of the sinfulness of a preoccupation with self."

"Your idealism is tempting. I so wish I could believe what you've said. Having studied the issues of state enough to realize that an ethic of *vivere libero*, preservation, is paramount I tell you the oughtness of a nation's rectitude goes down the tubes like the proverbial *'baby with the bathwater'* when a presumed risk threatens the state. Aside from those wrongs customarily attributed to rogue nations, especially the ones we propagandize to serve a rising hatred in the citizenry, one then adds the claptrap of being God's selected people accompanied by an irrational claim granting ruthlessness without limit."

"That's very Machiavellian," Suzanne replied.

"And also very true."

"I would like to suggest a counterpoint, for while your statement rings true in several ways, I have some strong suggestions that point to a more wholesome approach to the problems of state."

"If you please, Suzanne, I want to state that my criticism of your idealism is not from the heart. My observation is meant to demonstrate that international politics and religion don't have a commonality we might wish or even expect. We're talking apples and oranges here, so why harp on it?"

"Glad you asked. Yes sir, I think I'm prepared for this one. First of all, your apples and oranges don't define the problem at all.

I say we suffer from a national cognitive dissonance. By way of explanation, we collectively suffer from psychological conflict, our beliefs call for peace but we simultaneously support military intervention."

"I'm sure you recall the times after WW II our nation practiced the technique of containment and avoided military action. It was during this time of containment that we restrained the outbreak of volatility among nations. It was the American Diplomat, George F. Kennan, who heralded our response to the militant interests of the Soviet. Containment and the negotiation component kept our troops at home during this period. The losses on both sides of the more recent conflicts are evident. Trade sanctions cause 'collateral damage', that euphemism for cavalier killing of the innocent. The nation said to be '*under God*' must shift the tide of violence."

"And who shall do that?"

"Those citizens who implicitly support war, by their absence of objection. These people have the ultimate control, one to exercise restraint, containment and negotiate."

"This is dumping the responsibility on the citizenry for the lack of a motivated Congress to meet its responsibilities."

"Better than the alternative. The citizenry should act."

This is the day I must pay the Higgings if I'm to stay. You're staying through Labor Day aren't you, Suzanne?"

"Yes. We've given little thought to post Labor Day plans. Do you think the time is approaching when we should discuss anything, you know, like us?"

"Thought you'd never ask. What are we doing, Suzanne? Are we becoming the proverbial Millennials, wasting away our God given lives in selfish desires?"

"Not if we take our book seriously, but I do hear you. We must make some decision about the future. What are your post Labor Day plans, Basil?"

"Love those direct questions. Oh, here comes Mrs. Higgings now. This is the time to pay the rent."

"Good morning, folks. You both look as though the summer has been good to you. How nice to see you Suzanne and Basil."

"Morning Kay. Great to see you."

"I must ask, is there anything you need for the cottages? We haven't heard a peep from you two."

"I could use some more bath towels, Kay."

"And that you shall have."

"Me too, Kay, and I need a new frying pan. The non-stick is unstuck."

"That's easy. Time for a new one. Anything else?"

"Everything is fine, and we're having a great time, Kay."

"Well, that brings me to the next subject then."

"I know," said Basil, "The rent."

"You guessed it. I have to ask. Do you want to stay through Labor Day?"

Suzanne and Basil exchanged a lengthy look. He nodded saying, "We've decided, yes, we'll stay."

"Oh, that's nice. It brings me to my next question. Do you mind a very personal question?"

"Try us," replied Suzanne.

"I only ask because I have a couple who are regulars every summer and they've called for a reservation. Actually, I'm fresh out of cottages. I have never asked this, but are you living together?"

"No, no we're not," Suzanne stated.

"I guess we can't help you, Kay. We're not co-habiting," Basil replied flatly.

"I'm sorry. I shouldn't have asked," Kay spoke apologetically.

"Let us pay you now," said Basil, checkbook in hand.

"Oh, thank you. Please forgive me."

Kay wrote receipts for the rentals and before leaving brought fresh towels and promised the fry pan.

━━┿ ┿━━

Suzanne and Basil stood hand in hand on the deck of cottage #3. Suzanne spoke, "After all this conformity to the puritanical past I feel like doing something risqué. Let's go for a swim."

"You mean like? Well, yeah, I'll do that."

"Look, Basil, No one is on the beach."

"Hey, I'm ready, Suzanne."

"Let's just dare to this one time."

"Okay, see ya in a minute, sweetheart."

Moments passed as they readied and the two raced to the water's edge, sans suits. Basil trailed Suzanne.

"We must exersize that wondrous restraint they speak of, Basil."

"I want to hold you right now."

"Catch me if you can, Basil."

"Don't run so fast! Please Suzanne."

He caught her at the water's edge. They embraced.

━━┿ ┿━━

Kenneth Higgings stopped his SUV near cottage #3 and slipped out. The young nudists ran for the cottages when they caught sight of his vehicle. They mistakenly assumed he hadn't seen them as they dashed inside.

Higgings knocked on the door of cottage #3. A moment passed. Basil opened up, "May I help you?"

"Hi. You must be Porter. I'm Kay's husband."

"You're Kenneth. I saw your name on the rental papers," Basil replied modestly as they shook hands.

"Hope I haven't disturbed your beach party," Ken grinned, adding, "Kay and I want to invite you two out for a cruise"

"Let me ask Suzanne," Basil reddened as he led Ken to cottage #4.

"This is Mr. Higgings, Suzanne. He and Kay have invited us for a cruise"

"Hi Mr. Higgings. Yes, I would love to," she said, shaking hands.

"Can you be at the Sandwich Marina dock by two o'clock?" Ken asked.

"Most definitely. Yes sir, we're delighted," said Basil.

"We'll meet you. It's a 38 footer named *Eudemonia*. Bring a change of clothes and a bathing suit," Ken called as he returned to his SUV.

"I had no idea they owned such a big boat," declared Suzanne.

"Well, why not. They own these cottages," said Basil.

"I know that, silly, but Kay told me he's an ordained minister."

"What's he do?"

"She said he works as an interim pastor and visits people at Hospices."

⊷⊶

"This is really nice of them," Basil exclaimed as they neared the Town Landing.

"We need a break from our bookishness; what incredibly good fortune," she said slipping her Jeep into a shady spot.

Basil shouldered their duffels as they walked briskly to the docks. He scanned the pier commenting, "I don't see any big power boat here."

At that moment Kenneth stepped onto the wharf from his sloop, *Eudemonia*.

"You know what, Kenny? We were looking for a power boat. What a beautiful sloop."

"You're going to like it. Welcome aboard. Kay's in the galley preparing a snack."

They boarded and followed Ken below. He led them aft to the master suite, saying, "Just toss your duffels anywhere."

"This is so nice and so very plush," Suzanne exclaimed.

"We like it, Suzanne. This is our home away from home. Come on forward."

Kay greeted them, "Here, sit down and rest. You've got nothing to do until we cast off."

"I'll bet you're good sailors; am I right?" asked Kenny, winking broadly.

"I think we may qualify. Suzanne's sailed at Lake Superior."

"Where have you sailed, Basil?" Kay asked.

"Mostly I've worked on fishing rigs out of Gloucester. Haven't sailed a lot, but I've crewed on some rentals."

"You two sound like blue water sailors. Chances are we'll confine ourselves to local waters. Tell you what, we'll cast off and exit here at the east end of the canal and then head 'down-east' as they say for a bit. Have I missed anything?"

"We can't sleep over in the master suite," Suzanne whispered.

"Kay, I must have forgotten! Love the suspense, don't you?" Kenny's raucous laugh filled the cabin.

"Pay no attention to Kenny. He's had his fun. You two will have the separate bunks forward. Ken and I will sleep in the suite."

"You folks are so good to us, Kay," said Suzanne hiding tears.

Ken's on-board ship's clock struck reminding him to get under-way. "Hey Basil, you stand by to cast off the bow line. Kay will get the aft. I'll get her started."

Departing the marina was effortless. Capt. Kenny swung the *Eudemonia* hard east leaving a light column of smoke from the diesel's power surge. Minutes later they were in open water just outside the Cape Cod Canal's east end.

⚓

"The tide's running now so we'll buck some light rollers until we gain some distance from shore," Kenny advised.

By late afternoon *Eudemonia* had found the wind and tacked strongly ENE. Kay and Suzanne braced their deck shoes against the portside seats and watched Plymouth Town's sparkling shore lights.

Capt. Ken, knew of an ideal destination. "I know of a cozy cove a few miles from the Provincetown Light on the north side. There's a nice beach and is perfect for mooring *Eudemonia*. What say we anchor there until morning?"

"Couldn't suit me better, Kenny," cheered Basil.

"Running in the dark isn't my favorite thing. Whoever has the wheel is on watch," Capt. Ken said sternly.

"Oh, pshaw, Kenny. Stop harassing these two with your on-call demands. You and I can sail this bucket and you know it!"

Eudemonia's glass smooth hull sliced across Cape Cod Bay.

⊷ ⊶

"Tell us a little about yourselves," Capt. Ken urged.

"We met at the Coffee Shop in East Sandwich. Basil had stopped for lunch. The very next morning we surprised one another when we found we were both staying at the cottages," said Suzanne.

"Kay tells me you're both recent grads and members of the *Millennial* set."

Basil broke in, "We are *Millennials* and we're making an effort to disprove the accusations in the press and other places deploring our collective unworthiness!"

"We've heard of what you speak. What exactly is this effort of yours?"

"Well, first off, we found a mutual desire to write and what's happened, actually a possible beginning is in Suzanne's laptop. Now," Basil continued, "We've put all our thoughts there and let me tell you that it stands proudly to refute any negative crap the anti-millennials have to say."

"Sounds a little like us-versus-them," Kay added.

"We aren't bomb-throwers Kay, but with our book we hope to attain some understanding and respect. When you have the time I'd be happy if you would read what we've done," said Suzanne.

"Thanks. Later, because neither of us can read on the boat. Makes us upchuck. Have you planned beyond the summer, like your ambitions for later on?" Ken tossed the question casually.

"Oh, boy," sighed Basil, "in truth, we got so busy writing and exploring sand dunes all the rest is swim, eat and sleep."

"I guess you could say that we have no plans other than to do the book. Isn't that about it, Basil?"

"That's right, Suzanne," Basil said pensively, "but I have one other thing."

"What's that, Basil?" she asked.

"My plan is to ask you to marry me, sweet heart!"

Kay and Ken exchanged glances and exited the cockpit as quickly as decorum permitted. As they made their way to the galley Kay whispered, "Now, don't you say a word, Ken!"

Suzanne at a loss, finally found words, "Oh Basil, here we are out to sea in the night on a rolling boat and now you ask."

"Yes, and none too soon, either. Kenny saw us running around the beach naked. It's a wonder we're on this boat at all."

"I've news for you. I knew he saw us."

"Oh."

"Is your question still on the floor?"

"Of course sweetheart! Please tell me."

"Yes, I'll marry you. I don't know when I fell in love but it wasn't while you chased me up the beach stark naked."

A timeless interval augmented the ecstasy of the moment until a polite cough turned the couple's attention to the open hatch where Capt. Ken leaned precipitously.

"This is cause celebre. Kay and I congratulate you. May I have the privilege of conducting your ceremony?"

Basil got up grasping a handrail for support, "I think that would be just great. Thank you, Pastor Ken."

Suzanne kissed them both on the cheek, saying, "I must talk to Kay!"

Pastor Ken faced Basil squarely, "Neither of you have got your feet wet in this world. Do you have any idea what you want to do, son."

Basil felt a sting, "I want to give you a man's reply, Ken. The day of elders running everything is over. You ask my plans? Let me tell you about our book. The current Millennial put down is DOA as far as Suzanne and I are concerned. It isn't just us, you get it?"

The air was blue-black for a time. Finally Ken spoke, "That's what I hoped you'd say," he stepped forward and embraced Basil wih a manly hug.

Kay banged the dinner gong loudly, calling, "If you two can put your swords down, Suzanne has some words to offer."

"Love you all. Kay and I think a cookout on the beach would be nice, then a candlelight ceremony on deck if you all agree."

"Let us pray," said Pastor Ken folding his hands.

⊷⊱ ⊰⊶

"I regard this meal as sumptuous, Pastor Ken," said Basil locking his fingers and eyeing the food on the grille.

"We're glad to be able to. Most of the stuff we bring aboard is frozen. That large icebox amidships will hold for weeks. It was built to do that and has served us admirably ever since," Kay responded.

"Tell them what we do after the season, Kay."

"Oh, yes. After our last sail Kenny gathers up everything and delivers it to the foodbank downtown."

"This is a delightful wedding dinner. I called mom on my cell and told her the good news. I promised we would come home to see her soon. We couldn't feel better than right now here with you folks."

"I feel fine too," said Ken, "but I would like to draw your attention to the yonder clouds edging this way."

"Gotcha, Capt. Ken," Basil concurred.

"Let's decamp as they say. If we hurry we can stow the dory before the wind comes up," Ken added.

Clouds were racing to bring rain and possibly severe weather by the time they had bent a line astern and prepared to board *Eudemonia.*

"Let's get aboard now and see if we can beat the wind," said Capt. Kenny holding the dory firmly against the bumpers.

By the time they boarded an increasing wind driven rain was upon them.

"Too windy to stretch a canvas over the cockpit, Basil, let's just take things below," Capt Kenny yelled.

From the galley Kay shouted, "Feels like we're dragging anchor, Ken."

"It's holding now. Have to wait and see if she drags again. Come here Basil and let's give her a little scope."

"She tells me how to park too," winked Capt. Ken.

"Oh, I don't buy that Kenny!" Basil said laughingly.

"This is the switch for the masthead light, here. It's time, and now let's get the weather report."

"Here it is: _Cape Cod environs. Gale winds to 50 mph with heavy rain at times. Small craft warnings issued from Cape Hatteras to Boston. Heavy surf onshore. Next report 8.00 p.m., 2000 hours._

"Well, that's it. We'll stay on anchor until this lets up," Capt. Ken stated.

"A fine fettle of kish, Kenny! Here we are with a couple waiting at the altar and we're rained out."

"We can't do a candle ceremony on deck. I think we should leave it up to Suzanne," said Ken.

"I want to discuss this with Basil. C'mon Basil, let's sit down over here," said Suzanne.

The couple sat barely out of earshot of the Higgings. "Why don't we wait 'til morning. Things are bound to be better and we can get married then," said Suzanne.

"Gee, Suzanne, I saw Kay making up the master suite with all sort of nice things. Now you're saying don't even use it," Basil's glumness was plainly evident.

"Well, what's one more day? You've been trying to get into my, you know, all summer!"

"Because I'm a man. And besides, how could you tell?"

"I noted a total lack of restraint when we ran down the beach sans everything."

"Oh, Suzanne, Okay. You're right. You go tell them whatever you want. I'll go along with it," Basil spoke passively.

"C'mon Basil! Kay's pouring wine. Let's join them as guests should."

The four circled the pullout table. Kay poured chilled Merlot. Capt. Ken smiled curiously.

Suzanne spoke, "We've decided to ask you to perform our wedding ceremony tonight, right here in the main cabin with candles and all."

"Alright. Sounds good, Suzanne," Ken replied, "Write something if you like. Anything you want."

"It's agreed then, but it's so early, barely six o'clock, could we wait until later?" she asked.

Everyone nodded.

"You are an ordained minister, are you not, Kenneth?"

"Yes Mam. For a number of years."

"Well, there's something I want to ask and we have the time. I don't know if I'll get another chance, so may I ask you a question about religion?"

"Of course, and I'll do my best."

"Basil will confirm that during our talks about religion I'd developed a strong curiosity about Mysticism. I'm not sure, in fact, but I thought I was close to a mystic experience over by the sand dunes the other day. Could you help me because I'd like to understand more about Mysticism?"

"You're quite serious aren't you, Suzanne? I want to ask you, Basil, where does your interest stand on this rather special subject?"

"I never could get serious about Mysticism. Some say that people who get loaded up on some mind expanding drug may experience the same or similar vagaries."

"Your curiosity then is superficial, am I right Basil?"

"Yeah, I can take it or leave it."

"Your bride obviously has a lively interest. I will take her request and endeavor to answer within the allotted time, say an hour. I've never been asked this before."

"I want you to do it too, Reverend Ken," said Basil.

"I'll start with what Mysticism is, Suzanne, for that's your basic question. Several notables from various religious persuasions have claimed, as a result of their sense-experience, a supernatural presence. They have defined this as the existence of a divine reality transcending all sensations and ideas. The mystic claims that mysticism is beyond our perception of space and time, possibly another dimension. By the way, Mysticism is not confined to the Christian faith. For example, Sufism is the practice of Mysticism among the Moslems. Mysticism is also a practice within Hinduism.

"What does it require to have such an experience?" asked Suzanne.

"You're jumping several squares ahead with that question. The mystic experience is thought by many to have equivalency with conversion. That said, while conversion is held in awe, Mysticism has been shunted aside and often ignored amid claims of excessive non-rational nature. Mysticism is closely related to conversion, in that they have great consequence on a person. Certain experiences of

Mysticism have been accompanied by religious growth. Mysticism has been ridiculed as outside the realm of our current and most commonly intellectual and rational interpretation of religion. Another factor is called inborn inheritance, it's a kind of psychological influence within one's genome. It is often apparent within a person's temperament. Simply put, some are more inclined to a religious bent, perhaps a mindful desire towards religious experience than others. Early childhood training and the environment may also contribute. Those seeking transcendence may find their mystic path, one leading them to a land of the untouchable but real."

"My attempt involved me in a dizzying and unreal sense. I really don't know if I even entered anything resembling transcendence. You were with me, Basil, and I said I was dreaming and that it must be the air. I sensed darkness and yet we were in a sunny place," said Suzanne.

"Yup. I remember that. You said something about a distant forest, too. I would say we were about as dizzy as it is right now the way this boat is pitching."

"My first thought is to not try so hard. Transcendence isn't won by effort. If it's meant to be, then it'll occur. Something you might consider is whether a self-deception exists within our Christian beliefs, namely if our beliefs are absolute and stand free of the mystical experiment. The question has been raised before, whether Mysticism contains elements meriting inclusion within the Christian concept."

"I think I may understand what you've said Ken, but I don't get it; why if notable individuals have experienced and embraced the sanctity of Mysticism, then why hasn't it gained universal acceptance?" asked Basil.

"It has its critics. The non-rational element within Mysticism is a stumbling block. Another is a downright claim of perpetuated fraud. Do you know who some of the luminaries are who have claimed the mystic experience?"

"No, I don't think either of us do, Pastor Ken. I became interested in it during my religious seminars, and I've kind of pulled Basil into it with my own budding interest."

"I want to mention some of them. I expect that both of you will develop your own opinion of Mysticism on its merits and perhaps decide which camp you're in."

"I want to interject something before you name names, Pastor. I'll bet mystics over the centuries have been a tiny percentage of those of the Christian faith. I'm assuming that their miniscule numbers have lent support to those negatives you've described."

"Good point, Basil. You're right about the numbers and I agree that your premise is at the least a contributing factor."

"Wouldn't it be fair to say though that multitudes may have experienced Mysticism, but haven't been counted along with the known minority?" Suzanne asked.

"My guess is yes, very likely."

"That sounds to be radically distant from our current interests," said Suzanne.

"You're an inquiring pair and both wrongfully characterized Millennials. What I see are two young self-starters both holding Christian beliefs, and who, perhaps accidentally, have scratched the hidebound surface of establishment ideas within the religious community."

"You've made that into a kind of challenge, Ken. I'm almost afraid that my bride to be will take up the cause."

"I can recall many notable mystics and every time I do this I ask myself why the element of doubt exists. These are devout people. We favor reason today, and as a consequence we've outgrown some traditions and honored superstitions have been largely pigeonholed. In a sense we have suppressed out souls and that of others."

"I'm not at all sure we're ready for anything judgmental, Pastor Ken."

"The way this storm is progressing I'm more inclined to side with Noah and look for some animals to take aboard.," said Basil carefully maintaining his balance on his way to the head.

"What should we do, Pastor Ken?"

"I would follow my interests, Suzanne. Some who follow the Mystic Way and perseveres will in all probability reach his goal of union with God. Certain disciplines will serve as an enabler. A mystic's value system differs from that of the majority of us in that usually his or her temperament sets one apart. The tradition of your beginnings will influence your illumination if it isn't at variance with the orthodoxy of your group. Your progress may be exceedingly slow. You see, Suzanne, it's complicated. My recommendation tonight is for you to get up around this table, light all the candles and marry Basil."

"I have something I wish to show you, Pastor Ken." Suzanne handed him a closely handwritten page.

"This looks to me as if you've written you own wedding ceremony, Suzanne. Does Basil know about this?"

"Not exactly. You see, I don't know how to say it, but, I kind of, I guess I prayed that Basil would ask me, so I wrote this one night. I wanted to have something of our own."

"Kay! Come look at this. It's good. Read it, would you Kay? I think it's really good," said Ken.

Basil arrived back at table, glanced around and asked, "I'm missing something, aren't I people?"

Pastor Ken said, "I think your bride has been withholding this, Basil. It is a lovely worded wedding ceremony," he added, "Here, come on and read it."

"This is nice, Suzanne. Let's ask Pastor Ken to use it," Basil hugged Suzanne.

"Well, that's really good," Pastor Ken smiled, "I'll just add the required boiler-plate. No contingencies, no pre-nups right?"

Kay went on lighting several candles which emitted an ambience befitting the occasion.

"Time out people, I'm going to brush the bride's hair now," she busily exclaimed brandishing a comb and brush. Then you can proceed with the ceremony," said Kay.

"Okay Kay, we'll wait," Kenny responded, "I have to ask, Basil, your religious persuasion is Christian?"

"Oh yes sir, but I should add, Pastor Ken, that my piety has been shown to be somewhat lacking. My dear Suzanne is modestly more devout, I'm sure," stated Basil.

"We shall celebrate the Eucharist first. Then it will be our pleasure to share the reading of this lovely ceremonial commitment Suzanne prepared."

The service proceeded splendidly. The roaring of the winds and incessant ship's roll seemed diminished during the adoring ceremony. The Higgings congratulated and toasted the newly married several times offering many loving words. The newlyweds thanked Pastor and Mrs. Higgings profusely. Finally the four found themselves talked out.

Pastor Ken got up and stated plainly, "I think Kay and I will make our way to the forward bunks. If you need anything just help yourself." And with that, the pastor and Kay retired forward carrying their newly filled glasses. Kenny asked his wife, "What is that sign people hang on boats? *'If it's rockin don't bother knockin'*"

She hastily admonished him, "You're the kind of guy that hangs bells on bedsprings, Kenny," as they shared a moment of devilish laughter.

Eudemonia swung lazily, nearly motionless, in the cozy anchorage. Capt. Ken sounded eight bells while whispering softly *'Morning has risen'*. Kay's completion of her early matins led her to prepare a breakfast buffet in the galley. The newlyweds slipped along the master suite gangway and hit the deck carrying beach towels for an early dip.

Capt. Ken in absence of thought greeted the couple, "Have a good night?" Struck instantly by his tactless greeting he twisted to view the horizon.

After grace and prayer they ate as Capt. Ken suggested a sail plan for the day, saying that he had to return to Sandwich the next day.

Suzanne spoke up, "I'd love to visit the Plymouth Plantation. Isn't it across the bay?"

"Yes. Good thought. It would make for a neat cruise and we can return to Sandwich the next day. What about you, Basil?"

"Never been there, but like to go, Cap."

Kenneth seemed perplexed as he spoke to Suzanne quietly, "You know it wasn't a plantation, like, you know, with slaves."

"Oh, I know that, Capt. Ken. It was where the Pilgrims landed, fleeing from religious tyranny."

"Tell you what, after we pull anchor I want to talk to you Suzanne about the book you two are writing. How about it Basil, can you take us to Plymouth?"

"Oh yeah, thought you'd never ask. Yes, yes!"

⇥⧓⇤

"Finally we get a chance to talk, Suzanne," Pastor Ken offered her a flotation pillow as they settled down in the cockpit with a fresh pot of coffee.

"I'm delighted with our progress on the book. I've been hoping you would share some thoughts with us."

"My pleasure. I would be remiss not to. Give me more background on what you've done."

"Oh, good. Well, first I want to tell you that Basil, when we met, was preloaded with humanities' problems. He was, well, in a word, seething over the world's failure to have served our fellow man better. He has an opinion on everything. His relentless badgering about our need for social change triggered my interest so we went down that road writing about war, societal problems, religion, mans responsibility to the underprivileged, the affects of class distinction, and even the validity of Mysticism."

"You two put a lot on your plate."

"Oh, yes, but you know in many ways we're prepared to do this. My driving interest is to find a way for people to overcome their melancholy. I'd like to find the way so people can conquer whatever causes their depression."

"You *Millennials* are still fuming from that arrogant attack that characterized all of you as destined for massive greed and acquisition. It's an unwarranted cynicism and I'm sure time will disprove those iniquitous assertions. I'm right, am I not?"

"You're so right! We felt the sting renewed during our meeting in the *Coffee Shop*. Really, Pastor Ken, the *'Millennial curse'* ignited our cause."

"You know what I see? You and Basil are a couple of latent activists who've found a way to deliver your progressive ideas to others. But tell me, what exactly is your cause?"

"Basil told me when we first met that his ambition was to seek the wisdom of the philosophers and other worldly leaders, and his intent was to apply the answers to today's international problems, such as the Middle East."

"And you?"

"I came here to write this summer, something that would allow me to use what I've learned in my studies of philosophy and religion. The sand dunes here have a special fascination for me."

"But there's more, isn't there? You're seeking what then?"

"Is it possible, Ken? I want to broadcast a way to peace. I've made mistakes growing up. When I was a kid I was the neighborhood drug runner. Later, my boyfriend and I were forced into marriage because of a mistaken report of pregnancy. My quotidian guilt is all about his accident. He died at work while trying to support us."

"Guilt eats away at us, Suzanne. It appears you've earned relief from it. We've all done regrettable things. Now it's gone. It's irreparable.

You've begun a new life with your mutual interest in writing. It seems you're on a road to activism. If I may suggest, don't chase your inner peace. It will come to you."

"I have to ask you something right now, Pastor Ken."

A short shriek from *Eudemonia's* air horn demanded attention: "Permission to unfurl the genoa, Cap," came Basil's shouted request. Eudemonia felt the breeze and demanded a bone in her teeth. Basil enthused to grant it.

"Permission granted. Wait a sec, I'll take the wheel and hold her while you hoist."

Eudemonia's genoa snapped and filled. Her prow swung sharply as Basil returned to the wheel.

"I'm ready for your question now, Suzanne. Kay is joining us in a minute," said Kenny.

"Here goes. I would like to know, will there ever be resolution in our civilization for mankind to live in peace as so many religious leaders have sought?"

"So easy a question, so complex to attempt an answer. You've posited a question that has denied success to a myriad of collective opinions young lady. From the perspective of the Christian tradition the short answer is *Parousia*, the second coming. So many ideas have been submitted, but alas, there are also many negative views of narrow perspective, one of which declares the human race is forever denied the possibility of meaningful change."

"I found in my studies that certain composite identities observed within a tribe, a people or even a nation oftentimes manifest themselves as fear."

"The aspect of suspicion is provoked by a real or imagined potential that others possess to inflict unwanted influence, power or harm over the distressed."

"It happens in kindergarten."

"And also among nations. Fear can trigger a *Casus belli*, allegedly justifying war."

Kay Higgings slipped in next to them carrying a large plate with cold drinks and sandwiches. "I can tell," she began, "that you and my Kenny are into some heavy stuff. I want you to know, Missy, beneath his ministerial composure there beats the heart of a political activist."

"I'm beginning to sense that, Kay, and I kind of like it."

"Now that Kay has identified me for what I am, I'll put the facts on the table. I assure you, Suzanne, yes, I'm what she says, and I think Kay will concur that my norm to exist within the confines of my ministerial cage does mislead others as to my alternate interest."

"That sounds almost sinister, Capt. Kenny," declared Suzanne, "Actually, you should probably be talking to Basil. He's the political hothead."

"Yes, I recognized that. I have some ideas for Basil, but first I want to say that your manuscript shows a strong liking for activism. My guess is that you and Basil will find yourselves jailed somewhere for little more than refusing to shut-up while standing your ground in the public square."

"C'mon Ken, where are we on this? Isn't it better to stand for your beliefs during a public confrontation than remain mute, allowing your cause to be trampled? It isn't doing that much in the light of the risks taken by investigative reporters and journalists running amuck of international terrorism in war zones. Their perceived headlessness might even be featured on the evening news!"

"Tell you what, Suzanne, my take so far on our little talk leads me to think that you and Basil are made for more intrusive stuff than melancholy reductionism. Neither of you screw around when you're onto something."

"I think Basil and I have come on a little too strong and Capt. Ken has misunderstood us. Don't you agree with me, Kay?"

"He's been right before, Suzanne, but this sounds like it's winding into to a career decision so I'd be careful."

"You two are a pair, Suzanne. I don't mean that you should parachute into Iraq to confront ISIS. I'm thinking of a sensible and mature journalistic approach to expose possible dangers to the nation."

"You think, like you're quite serious Ken?"

"Why not? I've read enough of the manuscript. You write objectively. I'm suggesting journalism. You two have the killer-instinct to rally to a cause, like tigers out for lunch."

"Oh, Kenny, give this girl a break. She's a bride! We're going to visit where the Pilgrims landed soon."

"My Kay is right, Suzanne. Just disregard my wild ideas, but don't forget."

"Actually Ken, you've opened up a whole new vista for us. I can't wait to talk to *Commodore Basil* up there at the wheel."

"Hold on ladies. It's time for me to call the Harbor-master and beg for an overnight berth at dockside."

Kay and Suzanne watched the men drop sails. *Eudemonia* shuddered as the diesel kicked in. Capt. Ken drifted towards the quay as directed. The gals stood ready to slip the bumpers over. Ken slowed, reversed momentarily, sliding gently against the bollards. Basil secured the lines fore and aft.

"See that big restaurant over there, Basil? The white one with a big parking lot?" asked Ken.

"Yes sir."

"Well, here's the plan. Kay and I want to walk around town. We can meet you there, say 6:30 for dinner. How's that?"

"That's fine Captain, sir."

"You're welcome to come with us on our walk if you want, kids," Kay offered.

———

They had barely eaten their New England clam chowder, when Kenny struck again, "You know, Basil, Kay and I had a nice talk with Suzanne about your plans."

"I thought that was it Rev. Did you come to any startling conclusions during my spell at the wheel?"

"Oh, Basil, they were just talking about our potentials and stuff like that," cited Suzanne.

"I know, sweetie. I'm only chiding Kenny."

Ken continued unscathed, "Like the guy said, we're only trying to help."

"We know," said Basil, "I'm just tired and getting pretty hungry."

Kay interrupted, "Kenny, why don't we just hold this talk for another time," as she kicked him gently under the table.

"Alright, alright, let's talk about something else," said Kenny.

"I'd rather talk about whatever's on your mind now. Why don't we just get on with it?" Basil stated stiffly.

Kay spoke, "If I may interrupt, Kenny, I think it would be nice if you told our guests about your other interests."

"You know, Kay, I've been reluctant to mention my group's ideas in just so many words because I don't want it misconstrued as having a concealed motive."

"I could venture a guess, although I sense a total lack of transparency," Suzanne's hint contained a bit of fang.

"I can't figure it, there's nothing evident, so c'mon, Kenny, tell us!" Basil said.

Kenny was clearly in deep thought.

"I think I can tell!" declared Suzanne, "I bet it's about religion, and specifically Christianity. I'll risk all and declare emphatically that Kenny is thinking of baking a new pie."

Basil was shaken. "Gosh, Suzanne, how can you say anything like that?" he demanded. "When you were on my case you said something like '*Tell me, what really got you started on this track of the infidel?*' and you know that charge was way off base."

"Yes, I said that. I don't think you get it, Basil. Our devout Kenny is proposing to take up the revisionist's chisel to the Bible, like an update. I think he believes we're living in a bubble of historical fantasy. You know what that is? It's delusional and revisionist."

A silence permeated the dining room. Other diners exchanged polite smiles and quick glances at Suzanne.

"Pretty strong words young lady," Ken responded without rancor. "I want to preface my defense by declaring where I stand on the matter of the Bible's adherence to the absolute. What many believe is God's word has been edited, changed, re-written and tossed frequently to suit the whims of its examiners over the past couple of thousand years. Whole books were discarded when some astute group declared them to be inappropriate. That's historical revisionism Suzanne!"

"Stop me if I'm wrong, Capt. Ken, but it sounds to me like you're ready to push this through a sieve to filter out whatever you deem undesirable," Suzanne added boldly.

"Look here, Suzanne. I will stop you because you're wrong. I'm asking that I be allowed to state my interests to which Kay referred." Ken replied stiffly.

"Wait. I'm going to speak. It's my turn, folks! I suggest that we leave all these decisions and Kenny's declarations until after dessert and wine. Everyone, say yes!" Kay admonished with a tad of sternness coupled with humor.

"Yes, please. This dinner is a celebration of your wedding," Kenny said.

Silence again mercifully halted the hair-raising dialogue. Later a brief consensus about the food merged to small talk. More wine and dessert brought warmth and a desired camaraderie.

Kay asked Suzanne to please follow her. She did, and they paused out of earshot. Kay's eyes glistened as she said, "I must tell you something in confidence, Suzanne."

"You know you have that," she replied.

"My Kenny is afflicted with the early stages of Alzheimer's."

"I'm so sorry. I had no idea."

"I'm not at all sure if he is aware of it. He was diagnosed a couple of months ago. The progression is slow. Ken goes on the same as ever. I just felt I must tell you and Basil, so you'll understand," Kay said.

"My tirade accusing him of revision was insulting. I apologize for that."

"You did no harm. He will probably forget it."

They returned to the table. Suzanne's eyes were moist. She gave Basil a long sad look.

Kay recalled Kenny's talk of journalism during their sailing. She reopened the journalist issue by addressing Basil, "I've always thought journalism to be a fascinating occupation, don't you agree, Basil?"

"Oh yes. I watch and listen to all of them that I can. It's really caught my interest, not only the profession, but in the way they present the news."

"Then under all the gobbledygook we've been kicking around tonight, you agree that journalism is an important and respectable occupation?" said Ken.

"Well, yeah, that's why I studied political science so if I ever worked in the fourth estate I'd have a leg up on it."

"I find that your interests parallel a need of which I cannot overstate my depth of concern. I'm tremendously worried about our team of four."

"I missed something, sir, the team of four? Perhaps you would clarify," Basil knew his question was bold.

"Now I think it's time to divulge my alleged interests. Please hear me out. The team of four was formed about two years ago as a quasi-investigatory group. I founded it so actually we're five. The intent of this rather small and under-funded team was initially to follow the progress of new domestic legislation with an eye towards negative affects on the citizenry, such as minorities, like voting rights. Early on though the Middle-Eastern complexities captured our attention, particularly in the areas of the Holy Land" said Kenny.

"This doesn't sound anything like what I thought you were doing," Suzanne spoke apologetically.

"No, it isn't, and thank you. Now our group has reached an impasse. The four were in Syria. Later they fled the country when the danger level shot way up."

"This is becoming a story of pseudo-spying performed by what, rank amateurs? Am I wrong, Capt. Ken?" asked Basil.

"No, you're very nearly right. By the time the Middle East had our attention, we really hoped to acquire information useful to our government by using the pretense of an interest in historically religious happenings."

"It was a ruse, spying on another nation. I would call it espionage, plain and simple," said Basil.

"Well, somewhat, but our interests were never confined to legitimate governments, certainly not then."

"I think I get it. Now you're making sense to me Ken! What a magnificent ruse, your pseudo missionaries passing as Holy Land historians. You have balls sir!" Basil's attention was tight, his ego generously tweaked.

"Thanks for that. But, I've put these two couples in harm's way. They're much better as nosy historians than as international spies. Syria's internal problems got so hot they attempted to enter Turkey at a checkpoint where masses of fleeing Syrian refugees crossed. They were stopped and their papers withheld at that border crossing."

"How do you know this?" asked Suzanne.

"We received one letter from the Rollins and the Bauers a month ago. You may read it."

"I'm surprised the mail got out of the country, Ken."

"No, no problem. They're afraid of some sort of trouble and desperate to retrieve their papers."

"I must ask now; why tell us this?" Suzanne's unseen *Cheshire cat levitated* above the table.

"Here's why I'm telling you. I need to bail those four out. I know you could bring it off. Your youth and look of innocence is an enabler. Instead of shopworn professionals, your arrival as students of journalism sent to augment my small staff should diminish the customary surveillance that foreigners attract."

"At last," cracked Suzanne, "an honest job for two Millennials."

"This is only a rescue mission. It isn't even close to espionage. Their entry into Turkey was innocent. It's really only a matter of recovering their traveling papers," Ken said.

"I've a bunch of questions, Ken," Suzanne injected, "First, you don't sound like a preacher to me. Second, I can't imagine that we're sitting in a waterfront restaurant in Plymouth Massachusetts calmly discussing the recovery of foreign spies like we were talking about tomorrow's golf game, and third, just where are the mechanics of this? There is no plan! We can't just up and go!"

"I thought you might ask. Ministry is my second calling. I'm retired from government service. I'm going to tell you all of the rest tomorrow. Just think on it tonight while you're snuggling in *Eudemonia's* master suite."

"Surely you aren't suggesting we go to find them sir?" questioned Suzanne, clutching Basil's hand.

"Holy shit!" Basil got up grinning from ear to ear.

"Yes, that's about it. Now we've cleared the air. I know Basil, you are capable of '*in your face*' retort. I have to move on this. Otherwise my team could be victimized. I need a hardass son of a bitch with the daring to bring these people home and also a reporting journalist with all the savvy a guy can muster."

Basil Porter was ecstatic.

Kenny smiled at Kay. Kay said to Suzanne, "Remember Suzanne? I said Ken's a political activist."

⇥⇤

Conversation in the honeymooner's aft cabin elicited a creeping anxiety about any move to the Middle East. Basil clung to the temptation of adventure, although his cautionary reserve provoked him to ask, "How long do you think we can last in that country, sweetheart?"

"About as long as something else lasts, that's my guess."

Basil hesitated, "Oh! Okay, I got it. What I don't get is, here we're invited out on their boat and all of a sudden we've damn near co-erced into shipping out to the most conflicted part of the world as journalistic wannabes."

"Bet you never thought of it before. I'm going to share something I learned tonight, Basil. This will reduce your anxiety."

"All this talk about our great talent and stuff, I think it's a sales job to get us to really step in it. How can any rational person think we're equipped to do this? Is our fair-haired pastor real or is he whacked out?"

"I'm trying to tell you something."

"What's next?"

"Remember when Kay and I left the table? Well, she told me that Kenny has been diagnosed with onset Alzheimer's."

"I never would of thought of that! How sad. So, I guess you're say-ing that he won't remember it tomorrow."

"Well, yes. Gosh, Basil, I hope we're not wired in here!"

"I don't care now. You know, before you told me that, I was thinking. Can you imagine how far this would lift us up in this thing of international intrigue? We're looking at more than per-sonal gratification, this is nearly big-time. It's a giant step into the whole Mideast problem."

"Come on over here and whisper in my ear. Now tell me, Basil, suppose this is on the level, do you really want to do it?"

"Don't know. This thing is drawing me like a magnet."

"So much for pillow talk. I think you've answered the question. Anything else now?"

"It's your ear, I have an urge to nip it."

At nine o'clock Ken knocked on their cabin door adding, "Come on. Let's go to breakfast ashore."

Basis whispered to his bride, "C'mon kiddo, one more hug and I'm getting up."

Suzanne yawned, "Two hugs and I'll go with you."

Soon the four seated themselves at a nearby breakfast and lunch eatery.

Pastor Ken prayed, *"This is the day the Lord hath made. Let us rejoice in it."*

That moment deflated any suspicions of craziness the newlyweds held.

Sipping his coffee, Basil began with buoyant eagerness to recall the evening's offer, "I was wondering, Captain sir would you fill in some of yesterday's unknowns, you know, balance the equation for us?"

"So you are interested. Well, here's what has to be done. Locate the Rollins and the Bauers. This shouldn't be terribly difficult because the letter they sent said they are just avoiding going public. The letter said they're in a tiny Christian enclave near Sanhuria. They don't seem to know how to recover their documentation. As I told you, it was taken at the border crossing and I guess they panicked and followed others to Sanhuria. What I need is for you to go to them, give them the new credentials that I have and get them on whatever flights you can to return stateside. You'll use the Siirl Travel agency. That's your first order of business. Then your real work will begin, your career as journalists reporting to me starts then."

"We talked all last night. We know it's a career opportunity but the dangers make us very apprehensive, Ken. We feel we're plunging into a river of unknowns."

"I can make it more appetizing. First, it isn't a war zone. Your association with others on assignment is easy. Internet cafes abound so you're not alone. I'll detail how we can handle it. You can align with other reporters on the scene even though I'm sure you know reporters are notoriously busy people. You will be busy and drawn into situations and conditions requiring strict attention to the minor perils. All I'm seeking are periodic reports of crises; especially those of humanitarian matters and happenings affecting the refugees, the citizens, and local things that aren't on the evening news. You will interview refugees from Syria and Iraq, and also I want you to be of service to them whenever possible. My plan is to demonstrate to the world the disastrous results of these wars and your efforts to assist the refugees will be shown."

"We're fledglings in this world. Our educations are barely adequate to meet these needs. Our earning capacity has never been tested. Our book is all we have going for us now," said Suzanne.

"You're exactly right. This venture will put you where some of the action is. Consider it a fast track to professional recognition. It's going to put money in your pockets. It's your ticket to exponential growth."

"I like that word, exponential, Ken. Let's hear the rest, the money, when to go, how long to stay," asked Basil

"All expenses paid, plenty of walking around money, a generous down-stroke. A competitive salary with advance deposits in your bank account monthly. Life insurance, periodic pay increases. A minimum of one year of service and one midterm flight home and return. All in writing, kids."

"I'll tell you, we're stunned by the terms," said Suzanne.

"If I may interrupt we had better pull anchor. Ken needs to get on back," Kay rejoined.

The new heading was south. Kay took the wheel, enjoying a fine downwind breeze. Ken, Basil and Suzanne huddled over the details of the anticipated venture.

⇥⇤

Final preparations for the trip were mind boggling. Suzanne and Basil being obedient children visited their mothers where they found the joy of marriage converged with a love that only mothers could extend. The news of their sudden entry into foreign affairs was met with austere distraction, both mothers attempting to conceal an instinctive fear. On their way back to their cottage Suzanne cried silently, "I'm not sure my mom will accept what we're doing."

"I think we're asking too much of them to accept first our getting married and then going to Turkey, what they perceive as a wild and perilous move. After all, Suzanne, they both care so and want us to be well."

"We can call them from anywhere, right?"

"Oh yes. I think we'd better start calling them every day and keep on trying to relieve their anxieties."

"Speaking of anxiety my stomach is still rolling when I think we're leaving this week on our assignment."

"I checked with the airline. It's only a two stop flight. So far it sounds like a walk in the park."

"Don't you make light of it! I know where we're going and it's right into the borderland in Turkey. Who may become our neighbors?" She asked.

"We're gonna be okay. Let's just tighten our guts to the sticking point. Enjoy the excitement."

"Please Basil, don't go Shakespearean on me."

A knock on the door interrupted them.

"It's Kay. I'll get it," said Basil

"Morning Kay, c'mon in."

"Hey folks. I see you're almost packed. I've brought the rest of your stuff. Airline tickets, cash. You have a direct flight to O'hare. Then off you go. And you thought you'd loll on the sandy beaches of Cape Cod! Kenny is so pleased you'll rescue our friends."

"We're up to the challenge now, Kay. And, say these new phones are great," said Basil.

"I have to ask you Kay. How can Kenny handle these things. You told me he has Alzheimer's. Are we safe doing all this?"

"Its progression is slow. He's good and at his best doing just what he's doing, but I'll monitor the whole operation and you'll hear from me immediately of any change in Ken."

"These people, the Rollins and the Bauers; are they aware of Ken's situation?"

"Yes indeed. Dr. Bauer and Russ Rollins are specialists in mental health. This trip of theirs to the Holy Land was kind of an escapade. Their intention is to open a clinic treatment center to serve people with problems like Kenny's and study ways to combat Alzheimer's."

━‡‡━

Our Lufthansa flight touched down at Istanbul Ataturk, smoothly and without incident, but for one genuine surprise. Arrival clearance was performed strictly but routinely. Suzanne and I had reached the baggage pickup when she grabbed my sleeve, "Look at that sign on a stick. Look! That man is pushing toward us!"

I looked. There it was: '*Welcome Basil and Suzanne*'.

We stood there momentarily transfixed as the man wormed his way through.

"Hi! I'm Skip Secyev. Kenny sent me," Secyev's firm 'grip and grin' dissolved our apprehension. We were struck by his easygoing manner like he was about to ask us to lunch. After brief introductions that happened.

Basil spoke quietly to Suzanne at an opportune moment, "Kenny never said anything to me about this guy, Secyev."

"Me neither. Maybe he forgot. I guess we have to play it out," Suzanne replied as Secyev returned.

"Let's get some lunch. Here, I'll help you with your bags. I want you to meet some folks," Skip announced.

We followed Skip and our baggage to a restaurant within the plaza. He lead us directly to a table where two couples sat smiling broadly.

"You know what I think, Suzanne?"

"I do. It's gotta be them," she replied.

About halfway through lunch we had shed our presentiment of doom. Russell and Valerie Rollins and Dr. Mark Bauer and his wife Julia produced a thumbnail sketch of their tour and misfortune entering Turkey at the Syrian border crossing. I opened my attaché case and handed the new papers to them, the ones Ken had asked me to give them, saying "Ken sent these papers for you."

"No need, Mr. Porter," said Dr. Bauer, "Mr. Secyev here has found and generously delivered our traveling papers."

They were profuse in thanking Skip who had retrieved and returned their papers.

A second later Suzanne tapped my ankle and whispered, "Don't look, but that man in the dark suit by the door was watching when you opened your briefcase."

I glanced. I'm sure he caught my look. I could have sworn he gave me a masked wink. By then Suzanne and I had relaxed, actually swinging with it and thoroughly enjoyed our first meal of Turkish cuisine. Later we found that our new friends had their boarding passes and would begin their flight stateside that afternoon.

"I have to leave," said Skip, "You all chat for awhile if you like." He leaned over to Basil and said, "When you're ready to leave rent a car and drive to the Istanbul Marriott Hotel Sisli. It's not far and you already have a reservation. The internet is free and so's the parking. I must talk to you. Tonight is good for me, say around nine?"

Skip's extended hand reached everyone. He paid and left. We sat with our new friends until they were ready to board.

"Alone at last, Suzanne"

"Let's rent a car and get out of here."

I was ready. We found a porter and followed him to the car rentals. We settled into our suite at the Marriott and enjoyed a needed nap. Later at dinner we indulged ourselves with sushi.

Basil asked Suzanne, "Why don't I feel strange?"

"Wait and see," was all she said.

Basil sat while anticipating Skip's arrival and wondered what he wanted. The room phone rang.

Skip asked, "Hey Basil. Okay to come up?"

"Yes. Please do. See ya," turning to Suzanne, Basil said, "Oh Suzanne, better rustle up some snacks."

"Yes sir. Have you noticed your chauvinism is showing?"

"Sorry. I was thinking this thing may last awhile."

Skip knocked and entered. Basil anticipated the customary grip and grin, but no, Skip's countenance revealed a man whose earlier pleasantries were totally absent. His extended hand offered a note. It read: *'This room is bugged. Let's go for a walk. We'll talk along the way.'*

The note intimidated the junior journalists. The risk of possible surveillance demanded conversational gaps and reduced sensible repartee. Suzanne read the note, hesitated a moment, gave Skip a hug and her response, "Hi. Why don't you guys go for a walk. I'm bushed, I think I'll hit the sack. When you get back I'll serve the wine. It's chilling in the fridge."

"Great idea, Suzanne. I want to show Basil a bit of the city," said Skip stepping out of his shell.

"Can I bring anything back, sweetie?"

"Sure thing, rustle up some snacks." Basil caught the barb.

We sauntered through the lobby and hit the sidewalk. Basil had to ask, "How did you know our rooms are bugged?"

"I didn't. I wrote the note before I came. How did I know then? It's my pocket sensor. It picks up any of those pesky devices and responds."

"Why us, Skip?"

Skip's broad smile reappeared, "Hey Basil, get used to it. I made your reservations two days ago. This is standard surveillance procedure. Don't worry, no one's going to stab you in the elevator."

We walked. My attention was drawn to the bright lights, the stores and the scale of activity, then Skip's opener cut right to the bone, "Well, you're here. Now, tell me, what do you know about the current situation?"

"Only what's on T.V. The evening news, reading the paper and news magazines."

"A lotta shit gets filtered out."

"Well, yeah, I've heard that," Basil couldn't anticipate what would follow so he said, "I suppose you would notice that more than anyone else, what being in the business."

"Oh yeah, I get that a lot. Well, you know, so many stories of well over a million refugees entering Turkey from Iraq and Syria. Some have seen genocidal acts. They've left their dead in the streets, a matter of survival."

"Susan and I are supposed to interview refugees and furnish facts for Kenny's broadcasting."

"This is exactly what he told me. Ken and I were on the internet. He told me about your assignment and also your interests in book writing. In some ways you're extremely fortunate to hitch up with Kenny. I know what he wants, some facts on the cruelties from a humanitarian perspective."

"That's what we're to do," said Basil as they entered a park along the way. It was well lighted and quiet. The need to sit and relax provided some opportunity to turn some new ground about cause and effect in the Middle East. Skip spoke first, "Did you ever think you'd be here talking to another reporter about someone else's war?"

"My past few months is a genre of fiction, an unbelievable turn of events. You know what? The wheels came off my life when I fell asleep that first night in one of Kenny's cottages. It's been wild ever since."

"I can assure you my friend that you're awake. You want a genre of fiction; wait until we cross the border and spend a night or two in eastern Syria."

"You're not serious. I can't do that. I wouldn't take Suzanne near the place, besides I'm here to interview refugees, like people who got lucky and left."

"Then Kenny specified you couldn't leave Turkey?"

"No. Not exactly. He never said that. I'm not going to risk our lives though, not that way."

"He told me you had some balls. What the hell do you think we're here for?"

"This can't be. We're flying right back out of here. Besides, your story doesn't make sense. I can't believe you're serious" said Basil walking swiftly toward the park exit. He stopped short on the sidewalk, "Which way is the hotel?"

"Look, I'm your friend. Don't take off. You don't wanna get picked up at night."

"You walk me back to the hotel or I'll drop you right here."

"Watch yourself," said Secyev as he grabbed Basil's arm, "Let's walk."

Basil spoke as they neared the hotel, "Look, I didn't come here to get killed, and by the way, that Kenny, he wouldn't put us at risk!"

"You believe it? I'm not about to tell you. Here's a solution for a guy like you. Here's what to do. You stay in your hotel suite and I'll send you refugees. You can interview them over beer and pretzels and type your reports at night. No one back home has to know. How about it?"

"You're calling me a damn coward, that's what!' Basil took a swing at Skip but missed.

The curbside doorman gestured unmistakably and yelled in English, "Get outta here. Do it somewhere else."

Seconds later they entered the hotel nodding courteously to the doorman.

"C'mon up. Lets have a glass of wine," said Basil as they entered the elevator.

"Think about what I said, Basil."

"Which part?"

"Look, I can show you what's really going down. Forget what I said about staying in your room."

They reached Basil's door. He stopped, saying, "I've got to talk to Suzanne about this. I'll let you know."

"You wanna really do something, buddy? You let your sweetpants interview the refugees. She'll be safe here. We can do something really big, knock some of those suckers on their ass and do a real story. How about it?"

"That's crazy. What you been smoking, Secyev? Ken surely doesn't want us to get messed up like the Bauers and the Smythes did."

"You know where I found them? In a small Christian enclave barely within the country. The border guards wanted to return their papers but didn't know where those folks had gone."

"How'd you ever find them, Skip?"

"This isn't the time to be searching biblical sites I guess," Secyev's wooly reply triggered Basil's earlier suspicions.

Suzanne poured the wine and asked Basil, "Where did you put the snacks."

"Oh, right. Shucks, Skip and I got talking and I forgot."

"I want to toast you two for your courage to come over here. This is no ordinary war, folks."

"Is this our intro to Middle East 101, Skip?" Suzanne asked, attempting a touch of levity.

"I wish it was that easy. Tell you what. Take tomorrow and visit the city, do some shopping, buy a paper, talk to anybody you can. Stay together and get the feel of being here."

"That should be easy," said Basil and seizing the opening said, "Let me ask you, what do you do here?"

Skip's warbled some fanciful words, the classic response of a free-agent. A glance from Suzanne told Basil she too had picked up the aberration, Skip's deliberate failure to stay on point. Otherwise he seemed sincere and candid as he continued, "We know of many appalling genocidal acts in Syria. I'm sure my friend, Kenny, is eager for you to give recognition to those acts in your reports."

Suzanne again gave Basil a sly look. He imagined her traditional Cheshire Cat would appear.

Basil spoke, "Well, we thought that. I mean, just how do you get into the depth of things, you know, find the heavy stuff to report?"

"Ah, well, I have some experience as an investigative reporter, friends. I'm sure I can help."

"If I may, guys, I think what my Basil is alluding to is, do you find it necessary to cross borders and how do you do it?"

"But of course I don't. It's suicidal. Look, Turkey isn't involved in a shooting war and the nation's border is in tact, unlike Iraq's and Syria. I watched an American news showed recently. One could stand on a hill and watch the action."

"Of course you don't cross borders, Skip. Like you say, it's suicidal. I was only fishing. I suppose my assignment to report refugees' stories would be greatly enhanced if I crossed over so to speak," Basil said.

Suzanne was incensed, "I can't believe what I'm hearing. My Basil hasn't been in this country for a day yet and he's talking about jumping into a war zone to get interviews. No way, Basil!"

"Look you two, I'll deny that I've crossed borders. Let's stop this talk. Please, Suzanne, a little wine please."

Later Secyev motioned to Basil to see him at the door. Standing in the corridor he said, "We can't talk in there. You and Suzanne meet me in the morning, how about nine at the breakfast station?"

"Yeah, sure. Let's do that. Tell me, Skip, why are we hanging together? Kenny never mentioned teaming up."

"I'm surprised. Kenny always checks and double checks. Anyway, as he related to me, you two are to stay safe and sound right here in Turkey and prepare some personal stories about these displaced folks. Have I got that right?"

"Couldn't say it better, Skip. Seems like the Rollins and Bauers were very nearly our first refugees."

Skip smiled, "It's the intrigue of this business. Same old thing, don't count on anything. This interviewing border refugees is only part of the job. I'll explain it in the morning, but for now you should start to think in terms of a kind of reverse surveillance. I have access to stuff that, like you Americans say, will knock your socks off."

"Promise me this, Skip. Tomorrow we stop talking in riddles, I mean full disclosure."

"I'll use the most common weasel word known to man and you know it as well as I. Absolutely!" Skip winked and stepping into the elevator made his departure. Basil intuitively knew any search for absolutes was destined to oblivion.

Breakfast showed Skip Secyev to be more of a social animal than ever. He excused himself for a minute and Basil took the opportunity to speak his mind, "This guy is an actor. I know his whole performance in this dining room is for the benefit of anyone listening. He's B.S. made flesh."

Suzanne's whispered reply was spot on, "And exactly who is Skip Secyev? He's no journalist. He's a master player of some sort and for all we know he could be with Interpol, MI5 or even Mossad."

"There's a vagueness about him. He seems to live in some mysterious gray zone. You know what, I'm going to ride this out and follow the curve right to its asymptote."

"Explain please," Suzanne was puzzled.

"I'm going to move as close as possible to him and eventually he'll show his hand. I'll find who he really is without any intersect."

"You're serious?" She asked.

"Here he comes."

"You two up to a walk?"

"We're ready Skip, right Suzanne?"

"I'd love to. You show us around, Skip."

Basil whispered, "Are we being watched, Skip?'

"Can't tell."

"The park again?"

"Best place. Really nice in the morning. Here's the scoop. Sorry about all those lapses yesterday. First off, we all work for Kenny, right?"

"We don't understand, just who is this man, Kenny?" Suzanne asked, evading Skip's question.

"Thought you might ask. Well, I will say Kenny is so far up there that I'm not sure. He dabbles in international subterfuge like others dabble in real estate."

"He told us he's a minister, in fact he actually married us. Please don't tell us he's not," Suzanne pleaded.

"Not to worry. Where else could a former agent feel any safer. He's officially retired. I'll use the word cover but for the lack of a better word," Secyev answered.

"I don't like it one bit. It's terrible that man is operating under the pretext of being a churchman," Suzanne said with a generous smidgen of deceptive anger."

"He is a churchman. He just never quit his day job," said Skip, leaving Suzanne to apply her cunning act of mistrust.

"No, no, no! It's all wrong. I won't be part of this!" Suzanne acted aggrieved stopping short of cursing Kenny with obscenities. She sat on the grass daubing her eyes."

Skip Secyev looked puzzled, knowing his attempt to impress them with a fallacious description of Kenny having failed said, "Look, before you fly home, let me share something I've learned. We're working at a level so elementary that I can't believe it's actually within the intelligence community. Essentially you're talking a correspondent's game with just a tad of applied propaganda in the mix. You should be glad you were asked to play in this court."

"Then why you? Why us?" Basil demanded fixing his eyes on Secyev.

"Simple answer, we're unknown in the intelligence community. Like in tennis; '*advantage agent.*' Today an agent's identity may be as common as dead flies, but if he's unknown his ease of access can be close as your friendly neighborhood hacker."

"Please tell us about this clandestine correspondent's game you speak of," said Suzanne, her countenance fixed with pain and emotion.

Secyev said, "Here we go. Officially the job is to interview refugees. The delivery of deliberate pernicious propaganda is done up-line. Enough said. A flow of negative propaganda to known combatants can be accomplished in a very unobtrusive, but convincing way. Now, this is all you get. If you still want out I'll have you both on a plane this afternoon."

Skip walked ahead. Basil, looking incredulous, said "I'm as certain of this guy's credibility as I would be rounding the bases with Abbott and Costello."

Suzanne couldn't contain herself, "You're historically correct. I'll tell you now, this Skip has struck out."

Basil and Suzanne held hands on a park bench, "I'm sorry Skip, we had no idea of the gravity of our assignment. I'll go with it, but I'm concerned about Suzanne's safety."

Skip's reply, "The answer is that Suzanne is destined to interview refugees, the same as Kenny described. You and I have analogous plans"

"How safe are we, Skip," she asked.

"I like the way you phrased that, Suzanne. I like that much better than '*How dangerous is it.*' We will be doing this, like they say, in broad daylight. I'm not sure but what we'll enjoy concurrence in our host nation. It's possible that if your cover is blown you'd be thrown out of the country or worse. Of course, it depends what country or even if you're within a country. Borders shift at the whim of the victors. Some have ceased to exist. You see, Abu Bakr-al-Baghdadi seeks a Caliphate of territorial expansion, thus customary boundaries are victims.

"Long name isn't it? Who's he?" She asked.

"Can't tell you much except that the first Abu Bakr is said to have been Mohammed's confidant who converted to Islam some time before Mohammed lead Khadijah's caravan to Syria. He was named the first Muslim Caliph before Mohammed's death."

"You're suggestion that borders disappear, does that mean this job has a likelihood of mobility?"

"Not in the foreseeable future, friends."

"I guess it's decision time, sweetheart. What do you think."

"I feel like injecting some humor, guys. We all understood this walk in the park wasn't a walk in the park, did we not?"

"Certainly not a customary walk was it? When you're ready Basil, we can get together on the details."

"Skip will fill me in, sweetheart. You want to go shopping, spend some money?"

"I could do that. See you at the hotel. Now do be careful what you wish for, Basil. Kisses," said Suzanne. She exited the park flouncing with exaggerated motion.

⊷⊶

"Lets keep walking Basil. I'm going to tell you about an idea. Nothing at all revolutionary, but one where I agree with Ken. It has potential in that it opens the door a crack to instill a modicum of doubt in the listener's mind."

"I'm ready, Skip. You may tell me."

"You've heard of Jihads?"

"How could I not have?"

"I want to define something. Jihad comes in two formats either good, the higher Jihad or the lower, or bad Jihad."

"I understand that. The bad Jihads are the ones driving a mob controlled by tyrants using a twisted logic of extremism."

"Yes. We're going to involve ourselves in a good Jihad, one designed for inward-seeking and also to instill skepticism in the minds of madness."

"I get it."

"We're gonna give these refugees a voice and deliver it to the field so the tyrants' followers hear it."

"You mean propagandize."

"Believe it. What do you know about propaganda, Basil?"

"I thought I knew everything until now."

"First of all, get the idea out of your head that propaganda must be a lie. It is subversive because its intent is to undermine or over-throw something. It's also used to sell cars by telling the truth attractively. As they say, the saw cuts both ways. Emerson used the word *propagandist* as in the service of enlightenment."

"I think what you're saying is that the propagandizing pitch will carry the truth, at least as far as the authors believe and the will to accept or reject those inputs is determined in the minds of the perceivers."

"That's right smart, guy. A recipient of an input of this kind always considers the source, and the source is the author. You just now used the term author."

"Okay, a light just turned on. The authors are the refugees, and their stories are the message designed to instill doubt in the listeners' activities."

"Yes. And you see, the language barrier is essentially overcome. And what else does one need?"

"A means to round out the testimonies for the maximum benefit."

"And then what are the most desirable characteristics of propaganda to employ?"

"The main thrust of a refugee's story is the veracity conveyed."

"Absolutely. The plight of the refugee author must relate to the family of the enemy, like *'Is your family the next victim? How will they face your recent death?'* The truth is requisite to the purpose and the implied loss reaches in," said Skip.

'Ah yes,' thought Basil. *'the world's major weasel-word - absolutely, Skip!'*

"I'm in love with cognitive dissonance myself," Basil spoke convincingly, "I tell ya Skip my debates in political science prepared me very well for gaining the advantage."

"Try Demonizing them. Labeling them to blame for the disaster in their attempt at a social environment. Killing children, stuff like that.

"Another great propaganda ploy is to declare the falsity of claims made by the other side. Surely we've heard an adequate number of them. Try some on me, Skip."

I think they're all eligible. How about *'The American way is the way of the infidels?'*, a society of bottle blonds, something so easy to refute. Such a great idea, and it'll be broadcast, literally bombard ISIS at the frequencies they use," added Skip.

"I hear ya, Skip,"

"So, what do you think of the idea?"

"The truth Skip? The Islamic State is using YouTube and Twitter to their advantage every day. It may have worked for Goebbels, you know Hitler applauded the use of propaganda, emphasizing that the element of repetitive staying on message was the key success, but this is a different war and surely ISIS has made gains with them. One thing is that it's a very different mix of people many of whom are seeking a return to normalcy in their lives. Their idea is that this military action is corrective action, something very different that the get even psychology Hitler worked on his own people. And further the aggressors have a agenda that embraces the ideals of a holy war, like you said, driven Jihadists. My opinion? This effort you suggest is useless because it will not only fail to be internalized but will be totally rejected and likely to be the object of vulgar remarks by the very people who drove them here. Really this idea isn't worth a piss hole in the snow."

"You just dealt yourself out my friend. You may as well go home and watch the world go to hell on TV. I'm calling Kenny tomorrow. Consider yourselves off payroll."

"Listen Secyev, you just don't get it! Can't you see the folly in that radio broadcast? The ISIS are fighting to dominate the middle east, it's been said they will set up their own territorial caliphate. The refugees are the ones who got away. As far as ISIS is concerned there is no sympathy. Planning to change ISIS with refugee propaganda is worthless."

"Like I said, just get outta my face. It'll take talk radio to a new high and I'm glad you aren't part of it"

I thanked Skip Secyev for the lamb kabob lunch and found relief in a chilly departure lacking a handshake.

━━╋ ╋━━

I walked to the hotel. It was 4:00 p.m. I noted that our suite had been made up. It seemed I'd just hit the sack when Suzanne arrived and sat quietly on the side of the bed.

"Can you wake up? I want to show you my beautiful new dress."

"It looks real nice, sweetheart. You could wear it tonight. Maybe we'll go out later."

"We're going out? Sounds good. Where to?"

"I don't know. We can ask around."

"What happened? You're acting funny Basil. Did you two get your grand plans made?"

"Well yeah, no, not exactly. I got us fired. Let's sit down and I'll tell you,"

Basil related Skip's incompetent plan and sensed the growing presence of that '*Cheshire Cat*'.

"I don't like that man anyhow. Did Kenny ever mentioned him to you?"

"No, but Secyev certainly knows who Kenny is."

Basil outlined Skip's entire program. After a moment Suzanne broke a funereal silence, "You think something's wrong with this picture? Do you mean because Kenny, the spy who found God, sends us here without nary a clue of what to do and then Secyev, *whoever he is*, moves in and pushes such craziness, a thing Ken never mentioned?"

"I get it Suzanne! The cognitive term is '*whoever he is*'. We're going to find that out very soon. I'm calling Kenny."

"I want to interrupt this program for breaking news, Basil. Demand from the great Kenny just what game we're playing. We must know who this Skip Secyev is!"

"Okay. Right now," Basil said dialing out.

"Higgings speaking."

"This is Basil Porter, Ken."

"I'm glad you called, Basil."

"We've met with a problem and need your help."

"Have you been detained? Tell me."

"No, no, not like that. A guy met us at the airport. He seemed to know you well and he helped the Smythes and the Bauers with their papers and introduced us to them."

"Who did he say he is?"

"Name's Skip Secyev. That's all we know."

"I know him well enough, but by repute. Has he given you any trouble?"

"Not exactly, but he tried to rope me into some cockamamie scheme sending propaganda messages by radio to ISIS."

"Let me explain something, Basil. Hey, put Suzanne on the line first."

"She's on now."

"Hi Suzanne. You two just got there and already you're messed up with a pariah of the international shadow class. I want you both to hear this because I'm going to fill you in on some details about Secyev."

"Good Kenny. We're eager to hear it. I'm very worried," said Suzanne.

"He's kind of a rare cat because he works for himself and sells to anyone. He's a freelance spy. You can characterize him as a self employed mercenary with an attitude. By the way, his real skill, I'm told, is he's a master of cryptography."

"Does that have anything to do with radio transmission or things like that?" Suzanne questioned.

"Oh yes it does. Cryptography deals with the process whereby a message is covered by encoding sometimes called ciphers or enciphering. He's an expert, in fact he's developed some enciphered code that even further hides the message by the use of transposition or substitution or both. I think I can guess your next question."

"I guess you know, Secyev nearly talked me into radio broadcasting propaganda messages developed from the personal stories of refugees. He said these were to cause dissension among ISIS and his intent was to sway some minds."

"I can tell you now it's ignoble rot. His game-plan likely introduces a certain augmentation which in probability is to encode information of any critical geopolitical nature to someone willing to pay for it. I tell you, Basil and Suzanne, that fits his modus operandi precisely."

"Gotta ask you a couple of things, Kenny. Are we in danger of him and how should we proceed?" Basil asked.

"Considering what you've told me, my guess is that he will fade away. He knows you'll call me so he'll look for someone else to dupe. Cancel the broadcasting idea. Let's try this; Record each day's conversations on a disc and just mail them, say, on a weekly basis. Don't worry about the language barrier. I can have that all taken care of and done in preparation for use in my American broadcast."

"This sounds very doable, Kenny. Any other instructions or advice?"

"Yes. Ignore Secyev. Skip is an alias. Actually Secyev is very likely an alias too, although he's used it for years. If he becomes a problem call me at once. By the way, he's notorious as the consummate failed actor. His efforts are evident in the dramatis personae of crashed shows. His stage work is little better with his tenuous ties to intelligence agencies but he does cross borders with amazing impunity."

Suzanne chimed in, "It sounds as though his acting skills are quite acceptable at border crossings and I want to say, Ken, we pegged him as an extremely social person and quite an actor from the beginnings."

"Please, no border crossing. Secyev makes border crossing sound like Uptown Saturday Night. I've heard through my grapevine that he prefers to cross at a town named Karkamis. It's an occasional checkpoint manned by Turkish guards. Please don't go near it. Commutes are perilous at best."

Suzanne was ecstatic, "Oh Kenny, I know something about Karkamis. I was talking with Julia Rollins at the airport and she said Karkamis is an ancient Hittite city. I think that is where all their passports were put on hold."

"It may very well be. Now let me tell you of a nice community called Gaziantep where you will find refugees. It's about an hour from the Syrian border and it's a favorite spot. You two will enjoy the hospitality of *Starbucks* while you interview! Just get a roadmap and drive to Gaziantep."

"Wow! That sounds like our kind of interviewing Ken."

"Let's begin something, call me every other day. So long."

Kenny rang off.

⊷⊶

They napped for a while. Hours later showers were taken and the promised outing with meals eaten at a nearby restaurant specializing in fine Turkish cuisine. The newlyweds returned to their suite. Suzanne slept in a chair.

"Suzanne, when you wake up baby I'm ready. We've got the scoop on Skip and finally getting right with stuff."

She gave up her cat nap. "I'm ready now."

"We can drive to Gaziantep tomorrow and get this show on the road. Let me tell ya honey, it's good that Ken knew right away who alias Skip Secyev is. Remember the two couples our Skip befriended and then he introduced us."

"Of course."

Well, I'll just bet our little old buddy Skip works for Turkish Intelligence and that's why he could retrieve their passports, but wait, there's more!"

"I think I can tell the rest of the story."

"You very likely can."

"Remember when Skip advised us of our suite being tapped? What a laugh. He probably did it himself."

"Like Kenny said, he's an actor and he sure had us fooled."

"But yet, this is good, Basil. We've got a notch on our pistols now."

"I think we might call it a notch on our learning curve sweetie."

⊷⊶

By the fourth day of interviewing in Gaziantep both had acquired a fair skill in approaching the refugees. Sometimes they would find English spoken simplifying the otherwise immense difficulty of reaching the desired personal rapport to acquire sufficient bond and trust for a free exchange of words. They bought a lot of coffee and spent a lot of their *'walking around money'* to help loosen tongues.

One day, months into their interviewing efforts, Suzanne found Basil and spoke to him ecstatically, "You'll never guess how lucky I got a few minutes ago!"

"Kenny called and ordered you home on the next flight?"

"No, silly, nothing like that. See that woman over there and the young guy standing beside her? Well, I got talking with them. That's her son and he speaks good English and he said that his mom is a Sufi."

"I think I know what that is, but you better explain."

"You remember how much I wanted to try Mysticism?"

"Yup."

"Well, that is how she reaches God. Sufism is Islamist Mysticism."

"Are you ready to convert?"

"Of course not. Like Kenny said, Mysticism is a recognized practice in many religions, not only Christianity and Islam. But you see, she is what I would call a practitioner of Mysticism, and guess what?"

"I'll bite. What?"

"She and I are going up those hills over there later today and we'll pray together. It's like Mysticism 101 with a personal teacher!"

"Is the young son interpreter going?"

"Yes. Isn't this swell?"

"Okay. Let me know when and use your cell if you need me, Suzanne."

⟻⟼

"Remember that day that I had that nice talk with Hawiye, the friendly Sufi mystic?"

"Sure do Suzanne. She is a lovely person."

"She was. I've wondered what has happened to her and her son. You know they left the refugee camp. She said they would go, but I didn't expect them to leave without more notice."

"Is it any wonder, what with the daily dose of tragic family losses. She certainly gave you food for thought along the way. Let's hope she has found the solace she so richly deserves."

"That's what I want to talk about. She kindled a fire in me. I guess you know it. It all began the day we walked to the top of that hill and she and I prayed together. I tell you, Basil, her inspiration filled me with the dream I've had for so long. Not only the courage to continue to seek God through Mysticism, but I've thought so much lately about writing about humanity's relation with God, or to put it bluntly why is our humanity so lost at this time in history. Should I say during this time of the Millennial?"

"You've had an epiphany, and I'll bet it'll be in your bones forever. She surely awakened a spirit in you."

"Basil, you're such a dear. You do understand don't you."

"I think I understand that our ending of the book is likely to be a primer on humanity seeking God. I bet I'm right."

"You are right and you'll help me write it won't you?"

"I never thought I had a choice. Come closer little darlin. Basil wants a hug."

"I'm so happy, Basil."

"So when are you taking your laptop out of mothballs?"

"Today."

"You know what? I'm glad you decided to do this because I've always thought your religious studies at the university and your attempts at Mysticism are really where your interests are."

"Thank you sweet one. You know my heart belongs to God and to you always. I'm so pleased we can do this together and I know that someday you and I shall find our bliss."

"We're lucky now. These interviews are getting easier for us and this has been a world class experience. And we're sure Kenny is pleased with our efforts."

"We can do the writing at night so we can give our day job a full measure," said Suzanne.

"Have you decided where to begin?"

"I'm looking closely. People have always turned to seeking some sort of God or gods. I think my story should begin with the core reasons why they felt the need and pursued the unknown."

"You begin sweetheart, cause my Suzanne is the religious heavy."

"Well, the one thing that has given me an itch for a long time is that our humanity seeks to find or to know God and yet is frustrated in the attempts. I guess that's why I've been sitting in sand dunes and on the top of hills seeking a spiritual renaissance through Mysticism, but you know even with all of this I've never found it."

"But you've said others have confirmed they found God during those rare instances of insight."

"I know, there are those extraordinary claims, but at the opposite end of the spectrum we contend with those negative minds who insist that man is condemned to a life of emptiness."

"But just like you, multitudes have dispensed with the negativism and they continue to seek their bliss."

"I believe you're right, my dear Basil. Even those strong admonitions claiming man to be is lost, living in despair and only an accident of nature, man goes on seeking the truth. One will find in the myth of Sisyphus a fiction foisted on us by an otherwise brilliant existentialist philosopher."

"Well, certainly Albert Camus wasn't alone. Others in their assumed supreme wisdom have ascribed life to the pits, although in Sisyphus I recall that his fate was unrelenting, in rolling a stone to a hilltop only to have it roll down again and again. You could cite from Bertrand Russell, Jacques Monad and others."

"There again though, what man is so audacious as to tell others how to find God?" She asked.

"You don't want to hear my answer do you?"

"I'll tell you this. Every person who thinks in terms of a creator God must wonder if the revelation is innately within us, so therefore no other affirmation is required."

"But what of those over the centuries who have stumbled precariously among their own deceptive imaginings inventing their gods of choice with the appurtenances and contrived dogma designed to control their brothers and indeed even the earth?" Basil asked.

"My short answer? Man is not bound in his efforts or ambitions. Consider the incidents over centuries of war, inflicted death or deliberate starvation. Wars were fought over religious beliefs in which conversion at sword's point was demanded. I've read that land acquisition and other ambitions including the need of survival were commonplace within the ancient cultures of the Hittites, Persians, Egyptians, Babylonians and the Greeks."

"Is this entire program, the lives of men, nothing more than a work in progress? I could interpret it that way."

"Is it? A person may accept his religion of choice as the ultimate answer or one may consider all efforts in religion to be stepping stones along the path to the ultimate - that of God revealed," she replied.

"I was thinking of what a solitude it must be for those who assume the certainty of extinction to be their reward."

"My search has convinced me that it's characteristic of man from the time of the ancients to conduct an unquenchable search for and to the appeasing of their gods or God. And here we are, after thoughts of alternatives, man continues in his unconfirmed religions or his ongoing quest for God," Suzanne replied.

"A minute ago you said man is not bound in his efforts or ambitions, but I can think of instances where man can be bound up bigtime," said Basil.

"You're back on the tyrannical kick, right?"

"You bet. Remember, you studied religion and I studied political science. Many of us are deluged by religious teachings from an early age. It has been called the propaganda of infancy and as a result many are led to internalize and follow what they're told," he said.

"You're saying a child should not be proselytized. I can name any number of reasons why it is not only right but also obligatory and contains a sense of duty," stated Suzanne.

"Proselytize if you will, but have you not reduced the individual's right to exercise free will and perhaps performed an indoctrination that in some circles is called brainwashing?"

"I think it's a freedom and a right to show our offspring and others a path to follow, and what of free speech?" Suzanne's Cheshire appeared.

"We do agree that a person's religion is likely the most important thing a person may embrace?" He asked.

"Of course. That's why people proselytize."

"You know what, Suzanne? I just realized I was proselytized during my young years."

"And look at you now! You've thrown off that horrid yoke, that coercive brainwashing earnestly applied by well intended people who only wanted to save your soul. How many denominations have you tried since?" Suzanne said glibly.

"Can we call this a draw? I think our discussion has become circular in nature, so instead of begging for acquiescence, I would like to submit another scenario," said Basil.

"I welcome the change."

"Let me approach this power thing because that's what we are really discussing."

"You don't seem to have changed anything."

"I'm speaking as it influences the political spectrum. The power to control minds is handily implemented by political leaders to exploit a population by extolling the futility and purposelessness of life, or encourage indulgence in the superficiality of massive consumption, a supposed need to wage war or whatever radicalism will serve their leader's ambitions. Many, sometimes a majority, subordinate their lives and abandon their fate to the vagaries and ambitions of such a tyrant."

"I think what you just said is that the trends within society containing the potential design to lead people to peace can also make them susceptible to the whims of bad leaders," said Suzanne.

"I suggest you just look around and count the obedient rabbits among us. I rest my case."

"You know, Basil, this conversation somehow reminds me of our sailing on Cape Cod Bay with Ken and Kay."

"How so, sweetheart?"

"Well, we were driven by a strong downwind breeze and suddenly it ceased and we experienced a calm, what we sailors call a flat-ass calm. That's what's happening here; we're in a windless calm waiting for another breeze.

"Oh no, not you, Suzanne. I've never known you to be becalmed. My head isn't clearer than anyone else's, but when all is said and done my being says we must look to the source and that source is God, or whatever name pleases thou to call God. That's the well directed breeze to safe anchorage."

"Well, well, that's very well said for a political science person."

"But Suzanne, there's more. The word *acquisition,* is useful to identify many of the ancients you mentioned, even so, the word remains very much in vogue with many of today's world leaders. The clamor is for wealth and the road taken is control of the populace by use of a well known practice more recently called *manufactured consent.* This is an adaptation of propaganda specifically designed by an intellectual segment for the state or the moneyed power interests."

"Isn't this *manufactured consent* reserved for tin-pot dictators who hold control by violence?" asked Suzanne.

"The methodology is universally employed although it's perhaps more useful where constraints of violence are respected. The term *manufactured consent* has been around for a long time. Walter Lippmann is said to have first used it in 1921.

"This *manufactured consent* is a subversion of public interest, is it not?"

"Yeah, it's a fragile discipline designed to influence the citizenries opinion to align with the interests of the powers that be."

"You know what I see in our world? I see a war of words, words that are chameleonic like when the meaning suffers subtle or suggestive change. I think you are onto something. I wonder, Basil, if a different approach to the spoken word might yield more exact interpretation of the original meanings, know what I mean?"

"I'm thinking that the number of words, even limited to those in common use along with their roots enormously challenge mankind's ability to find resolution."

"It kind of dumps it all back on us doesn't it? I mean here we are totally dependent on words to convey meaning and you said the job of putting it all out there is likely impossible."

"I would submit to you that the term *manufactured consent* is of itself a combination raising questions as to its real meaning. Just how does one manufacture consent?"

"Maybe you should call in your mathematical genius and be very kind to your computer as you seek truth."

"You're hitting on something that might do just that, something really big!"

"Well, okay, I'll bite. What is it, Basil?"

"You have an uncanny influence, the appearance of a *Cheshire Cat!* I've always wanted to ask you about it. How do you deploy that insidious countenance of a grinning feline?"

"Oh, you speak of my *Cheshire Cat look?* That pussy is withheld from your obsession. My secret, Basil!"

"May I use it as a correlation?"

"If it works run with it."

"You recall Alice observed a grin-less *Cheshire*; saying: *'Well, I've often seen a cat without a grin, but a grin without a cat! It's the most curious thing I've ever seen in my life!'*"

"Everyone recalls that," replied Suzanne.

"Right. Anyway, my point is that we attribute certain unassailable characteristics to a myriad of stuff in life and those very things remain rock solid unless and until they're exposed to error."

"Go on please, Basil."

"Here goes. We've been in Turkey now for several months, right?"

"Yup, and I've learned a lot!"

"Of course you have, but now let me present my point. Tell me, how different are the people we've communicated with, those where we touched their lives, like the refugees we interview? Tell me of the great differences that separate us as a people."

"I see a great similarity, a likeness, something I'll call commonality among all of us."

"Okay. You like *Starbucks*. They like *Starbucks*, right?"

"Of course."

"I'll interject a word now; *innate.* You know, inborn, instinctive, and intrinsic to the human race."

"I get it Basil, but why then do you think the world is in such a pervasive and endless turmoil? Answer me that!"

"Thank you for that. You've opened a bottomless can of worms that I can't explain. Why not talk about the twenty-first century approach underway, you know, artificial intelligence?"

"I hope that our specialists practice restraint in making the computer parallel human intelligence. One must ask that the malicious characteristics of humans somehow be negated in yet another of man's control systems."

"I'm not at all sure it will remain man's control system for very long. You know the fear already persists that numerous processes within the AI system will in likelihood gain access to man's evil.

The upshot is that AI computers must not change its own source code."

"Perhaps AI could restrict man's differences to discussion and negotiation with inherent prohibitions controlling those irrational impulses so common to us."

"Suzanne, you are autodidactic. How do you come up with these ideas?"

"I hope my studies of psychology are evidentiary of the comments I've made, Mr. Bigword. How about you?"

"I'll depend on what's hidden by that shadowy veil of existence where one may anticipate the presence of the good, the bad and the ugly. My world is in there somewhere sweetie."

"Where does this leave you with your politicizing and control by government?" She asked.

"I suppose government may become a burden to society when our glorious AI computers run the world."

"When are we going to go to bed?"

"Right now sweetheart."

━┽╂┾━

"Morning sweetie! Did you hear the phone ring last night?"

"I heard you talking but I guess I dozed off."

"Well, I'm sure you want to know. It was Kay. She said that we're being recalled. He's recalled us!"

"What's happened? Why now, and what of our journalism career?"

"At first I misunderstood what she said last night. I guess their enthusiasm for our following a journalistic career was well intended but she said Kenny wants us to get what he calls a real world experience."

"We got that alright. In a word, screwed. We did our job, dealt with that jerk, Skippy, and we got the refugee stories for his program, whatever that is. So why?"

"Actually, I'm sure he's pleased with what we've done. She said just that."

"I repeat. What about our journalism career?"

"Actually Suzanne we're not journalists, not yet anyhow. I think Kenny did this to give us a heads-up, to help us see things as they are and to be resourceful."

"How charming of him. Kinda sounds like sponsored bull-shit don't it?"

"Yeah. But ya know, that's the way he really is. I'm convinced of it."

"You know the term grubstake?" asked Basil.

"Of course. Don't tell me he wants to leave his fangs in us?"

"Not exactly. Kay said Kenny wants to back us to put us on the road in our choice of work."

"And?" Suzanne's Cheshire struck a grin.

"No strings. Besides, we've put some bucks together here. We're not hung with government loans for education and we have money in the bank, Suzanne. Not bad."

"My frugality is peaking! Do you think we should thank him? So, how long do we have, Basil?"

"She said '*Take what time you need to clean things up.*' We just call when we're ready. By the way, you will let Ken live won't you?" Basil asked moving closer

"Oh Basil, yes, of course. Let's just stay here and snuggle for a while. We can call down for breakfast later."

⊶⊷

The last leg of the flight from Heathrow was daylight all the way and the connections were incident free.

"I'll call as soon as we land and tell them we're booked through to Hyannis today," said Basil.

"Now that you're a jetsetter you must say deplane, deplane. I wonder if we can have one of our cottages back for a few days?" she asked.

"I'll ask. You know, like they say, everything changes but nothing changes."

"There is one change I've meant to mention, Basil."

"What?"

"Pregnant."

"Oh! You?"

"I don't think I would announce another woman's pregnancy, do you?"

"Wonderful. Wow. I think I'll announce this right here and now."

"I don't want to rain on your parade honey, but the fasten seat belts sign just flashed and our hostess is eyeing you. Better fasten up and rejoice after," she implored tugging on his sleeve.

The hostess made a hasty approach to address Basil, *"Please sit and fasten your seat belt sir. We are making our approach."*

As they deplaned at Boston's Logan International, Basil couldn't restrain himself so he attempted some wit, "If we had stayed in Turkey our child may have had dual citizenship."

"It's the first trimester so who can say? Our baby may hold citizenship in Timbuktu."

"Now that's something we could talk about. Let's check in for our Hyannis flight and get some coffee."

Their eyes met. "Look," said Basil, "My antics on the plane were because I was so stunned. I want to say before we go on that I'm so delightfully pleased with the news and you and you alone are the great love of my life."

"I'm pleased to have our child, Basil. We are as one, and I know we're forever," she replied.

"More coffee?" A voice interrupted their loving contemplation.

"Yeah, please fill it up," Basil leaned to Suzanne, "We have time before they announce to board."

"I was thinking how un-Millennial we are what with starting our family without years of delay"

"Ha! We surely have defeated the ribald accusations flung at us as Millennials. Have you noticed, sweet one, we have never entertained the call of Wall Street to feed our greed?"

"I have a question for you, oh great swami."

"Dumb looks are still free."

"Just where are we on the Millennial greed curve?"

"Us? We're so far from the asymptote I think the line refutes the rule. By the way, we never subscribed to the unpopular fixation some observers hold. I'm still pissed about it. The accusation is without merit, a malicious fabrication to belittle our age group."

"I thought you might say something like that. I agree. And we should board now unless you want to stay in *Bean Town* tonight."

They rushed to the boarding gate. Basil spoke, "Know what? We covered a lot of ground just now."

During their return flight to Cape Cod Basil spoke of how he looked forward to talking with Kenny and Kay. "It's been almost a year since we've seen them. Gosh, I should have called them!"

"Let me call, Basil. You said that Kay announced our need to return home and I'm wondering if something isn't odd. Why do you think she made the call?"

"Yeah. I don't know. I was gonna wait until we met them again, but go ahead."

"Hello."

"Hi Kay. This is Suzanne. We're at the Hyannis Airport now."

"Oh, Suzanne. Hi. I'm so glad you called. Can you come to our house soon."

"I think so. Let me ask Basil." A moment later she said, *"Yes. We can come over now if it's okay."*

"Please come over soon, Suzanne. Something terrible is happening and we must talk. Please."

"We'll be there as soon as we can get our bags and rent a car, Kay. Is there anything we should do before we come to your place?"

"No. Just come on over."

"Alright. Bye Kay."

"Your hunch is right. She sounded troubled. We must get right over there."

━┼┼━

Suzanne and Basil were silent during the drive, each seeking to find an answer as to what had happened to Ken and Kay.

Kay answered the door. Amid kisses and hugs Suzanne whispered, "We have to know, Kay, what has happened?"

"Come and sit down on the porch for a moment," Kay replied. Kay had been crying.

"Something awful is happening to Ken," Kay continued, "The doctors have told me the Alzheimer's is progressing."

The Porters were stunned by Kay's annoucement.

"Oh my," Suzanne struggled with words, "Is he at home now, Kay."

"Yes, yes. He's sitting in the living room. I just wanted to tell you this before we went in."

Basil strode across the carpet, taking Ken's outstretched hand. "Great to see you, Kenny."

"Glad you could come," Ken replied.

Their conversations that night disclosed Ken's current condition to be what the doctors had said. Suzanne and Basil had been forewarned, but hadn't anticipated how rapidly the affects were.

Basil talked in a forced singular fashion, relating to Ken the several experiences they had in Turkey. He noted that Ken's attention was unpredictable, advancing and receding from apparent interest to a momentary lack of awareness or interest.

Suzanne and Kay huddled at Kay's kitchen table, Kay's grief-stricken voice relating the first signs of Kenny's Alzheimer's, reminding Suzanne how she mentioned it during their sailing trip to Plymouth the previous summer.

"I guess I just couldn't tell myself what deep down I knew, Suzanne. I told myself it would go away."

The two women recognized the serious need for an in depth understanding of Ken's approaching difficulties. Suzanne responded with anguish when Kay told her of the ways their lives had changed,

"You know, Kay, I've had one tragedy in my life. I was seventeen and thought I was pregnant so the families forced a shotgun wedding. Well, my husband died in an industrial accident less than a year afterwards. Actually, I wasn't pregnant so I was a childless and a widow at eighteen."

"I'm sorry. I had no idea. You were so young."

"I must tell you something! I just told Basil today. I'm going to have our baby!"

The news cheered them as they clasped hands at the table. Later they rejoined Ken and Basil commiserating about happier days.

After expressing themselves and promising to return the next day they departed. Kay slipped the key to cottage 4 to Suzanne saying "I saved the cottage for you two."

Upon return to the cottage colony Basil spoke first, "This evening was without success. I am trying to make small talk with a man whose mental faculties were so great, and there I was with tears in my eyes hoping so much for his response. Damn it, Suzanne, it doesn't seem right."

"I understand, but you can't expect to change anything. And we were totally unprepared for what we walked into."

"I guess. What impressions did you get from it all?"

"What can I say. Their lives as they knew it are substantially over. I'm so sorry this has happened to Ken, and I don't know if Kay can handle it."

"Tell me, did you learn about Alzheimer's in your psychology classes?"

"Yes, but briefly. I did manage to read up on it and other problems like bipolar disease."

"Well, tell me, what happens to a person's mind or brain when they become afflicted with Alzheimer's."

"You want the whole megillah?"

"Just a nodding acquaintance thank you."

"Not while you're driving, Basil. Sometime when we're bright eyed and bushy tailed.

"Tell you what, Suzanne," Basil rubbed his eyes and noted he was staring at the ceiling in cottage #4.

"I'm awake. Go ahead."

"I've been thinking about Kenny and Kay."

"You don't say? You've been tossing around a lot."

"And you haven't?" Basil rolled close and gave her a smack on the cheek."

"Go on and tell me, tell me what?" Suzanne teased.

"First, we mustn't take any money from them. Ken's a sick man and whatever offers he made are kaput."

"Agreed. I wouldn't let you do that anyhow. What's next great swammi?"

"They've been darn good to us. I think we should do something nice for them."

"Basil, I want to say you're making a lot of sense for this early in the morning."

"I guess my subconscious worked last night."

"You've got it right. The subconscious is said to influence our behaviour and resolve some of our problems while we sleep."

"I've heard variations on that theme but I'll accept that. Anyway, what do you think we could do for the Higgings?"

"I didn't sleep well either and my waking thoughts went further than our visit to tell Kay how sorry we are."

"I like that. So tell me more," Basil sat up.

"You want the short answer first?" She asked.

"Yes. Let's start at the end and leave the details until after breakfast."

"First off, my educational background in psychology is preparatory to entering the field of prevention and I think I could get into caring for those with Alzheimer's and related neurocognitive disorders," Suzanne's eyes flashed with enthusiasm.

"Sounds like your subconscious worked overtime," said Basil, "It makes sense. How can you miss?"

"You bet it does, Basil! Let me explain at breakfast. You're taking me out, right?"

"Yes. Of course. I planned that all along."

⇥ ⇤

"Why not regress to our beginnings? I want to go back to where this all began," stated Basil, resolutely.

"You'll get no argument from me," Suzanne responded.

Basil rolled his Harley from the shed, saying, "Someone has kept my bike charged up and neat as a pin."

"I couldn't guess, can you?"

"Oh yeah. I'm sure it was Higgings. Jump on my love as we motor west to the East Sandwich Coffee shop."

"I'm loving it," said Suzanne as they rolled onto route 6A.

"Isn't this something? Do you remember how my adamant comments about *class* nearly severed a budding interest?" asked Basil.

"Yup. It was more than that. But you know what? I figured you for a thinker. One could say I was attracted to your mind rather than the bike."

"Wasn't it a bit of a risk letting me walk out of the coffee shop that day?"

"Not really. The only brochures in the rack of tourist places to stay were the cottages where I was."

"It was part of a plan then! Have you changed your mind?"

"Yes to the plan and no I haven't changed my mind. You know, speaking of minds, let's get serious about yesterday's ideas."

"Yes. We've gotta move on this. Right now we're Millennials with money but that won't last forever."

"Table for two, please."

"Welcome folks. Right by the window, okay?"

"Delighted. We're both having a caffeine fit, so please."

"Be right back," declared waitress Jan.

"Let's order and then talk about health."

"You know more than I do about it," said Basil.

"It's predicted that dementia and Alzheimer's disease symptoms wll double by 2030. At this time there is no known effective treatment or cure for it."

"That's a wakeup call if I ever heard one."

"Here's a bunch of stuff. They say that changes in the brain may occur, one's that may soon be identified, but as of now don't indicate symptoms. So, preventative interventions are paramount if and when indications of neurocognitive disorders show up."

"Are you really interested?"

"Yes, of course. What with the threat of potential memory loss, disorientation, and paranoia reducing us to total ineptitude, why not?"

"You talk like you want to get into the industry"

"I've thought of it. What do you think?"

"But what of the prerequisites?"

"They can be met. The how of it already exists. It's called the *National Alzheimer's Project Act. {NAPA}* has been around since 2011."

"Tell me what you do understand of it."

"Not much. I've heard it said that some basic lifestyle changes can influence the progress of onset Alzheimer's, and I have a hunch about it. Want to hear it?"

"Go ahead. I'm all ears."

"Well, to my way of thinking the sameness or incessant regularity of life's activity may lead to onset Alzheimer's. It's a maybe, but overuse or unused connectivity just might be the something causes a neurodegenerative disorder in the brain. It's a gradual thing. The most obvious and first noticed fault is declining memory."

"You think that if a person changes their activity and reduces the repeatability of stuff that it could be a factor?"

"I've thought about it, but yet most say that the contributing causes are not well known."

What of genetics? Aren't some people much more susceptible?"

"Yes. And it's also likely that a whole array of risk factors exist."

"You've thought about this haven't you?"

"Oh, yes. And I can tell you that some really bizarre appoaches are in consideration. One is a non-evasive neural implant."

"You've reached the limit of my congruence sweetie, but I have a question. Your interests seems renewed at the very least. Would you be this interested if Kenny had no indication of the disease?"

"Probably not. Have you thought how much attention a person gives to any problem until it knocks at their door? Hearing of Kenny's situation certainly rang a bell."

"And now you're weighing in on it, right?"

"Yes. But I also know, Basil, that we're facing a crisis ourselves. Kenny's got his and we have ours, you know, what's called decision time."

"I'm going to be blunt, Suzanne. I'll do anything I can for Ken and Kay, and I'll always support you, but my personal objective is mathematics. It's always been my thing."

"I know that and you should do it. The way I see it the journalism ride was exciting but not for us. It's been thrilling, now it's over. Like they say, a blip on the screen."

"Kenny really gave us a great opportunity. He helped us a lot."

"And in a sense he's now coincidentally caused us to hear that rap on the door, to consider a career in one of the biggest health challenges of any generation, insidious dementia."

"I want to talk to Ken again. You want to make another visit? I'll call Kay and see if we can go over," said Basil.

"Yes, sure. Call. Suzanne engaged Jan in small talk, telling her how she had worked part time at the Coffee Shop until one day when Basil showed up for lunch."

━┼┼━

"Kay said to come for lunch," Basil relayed from the Coffee Shop entrance."

"Well, come on back. Let's talk for a while. Have you decided yet on what you'll do in your remaining years?" Suzanne giggled as she toe tapped Basil gently under the table.

"All I was saying is that I would like to use mathematics in my work. It's a universal language and I would like to apply it in science."

"I thought some more on what we were saying before about the mental health industry. It's a noble cause and I'm of a mind to look into it more."

"So, are you saying it's your list?"

"No. I just never took it off," she replied.

On the way to Kay and Ken's they bought some flowers. Basil handed them to Kay when she opened her front door.

"Oh thank you both. I'm pleased you could come to see us today," Kay smiled broadly but couldn't veil the pain she carried.

Kenny acknowledged the visitors with a wave and returned to the pensive melancholy of his recliner.

Kay attempted to bridge the silence, saying, "It's not too early for some wine is it?" She placed a decanter between them.

"Thank you Kay. I don't mind a little eye opener myself," cheered Basil rising to the occasion.

"I have some good news today. Both the Rollins and Dr. Mark and Julia Bauer will join us for lunch," Kay said determinedly.

"Oh, I'd love to see them," declared Suzanne, "It's been over a year. What are they doing these days?"

"You know their biblical history search was a kind of vacation for them. They were glad to get home and back to their work." said Kay.

"I know they were pretty upset leaving when we met at the airport," said Basil.

"Well, anyway, Suzanne, they're setting up a new facility, a clinic I think. The last time I talked to Dr. Mark he told me that construction was underway."

"How frustrating it must be for them. It isn't easy to prowl around a foreign country looking for ancient reminisces and artifacts from the past," said Basil, "and of course that other sideline Kenny called information gathering."

"Yes, and I understand the implied euphemism, thank you. I knew about it. Even so, they made some notable submissions to those seeking to expand on biblical history," Kay replied.

Suzanne interrupted, asking Kay, "May I help you in the kitchen, Kay."

"Yes you can young lady. Let's make haste. Our other guests should arrive soon."

Basil moved closer to Ken, "You remember me Kenny, I'm Basil. Gimme five, buddy."

Ken spoke, "How are you?"

"I'm good Kenny. Been missing our sailing though. We had a helluva time didn't we?"

Ken was searching, "You're Basil."

"Yes sir. It's great to see you again, Ken," Basil winced.

Basil attempted to exchange thoughts, but soon Ken's response drifted to silence. Ken sat gazing through the window. Basil was distressed as he gazed at his friend, the man who was his benefactor and employer. His composure crushed, he cried silently.

⬅✛ ✛➡

The door chimes mercifully broke Basil's plummeting spiral. The Rollins and the Bauers entered amid hugs and passionate cordiality.

Valerie Rollins happily greeted Suzanne and Basil recalling their luncheon meeting at Istanbul Ataturk, "How nice to see you. We didn't know you were back home from your stint in Turkey."

"We just got in yesterday, Valerie. We're happy to be here," said Suzanne.

"Good to see you both. Remember that man, he called himself Skip Secyev?"

"We certainly do," Basil replied darkly, "He almost duped me into a crazy radio broadcast."

"When we got home Kenny told Russ that Skip played both sides of the street. That Secyev is a dangerous man."

"Yeah, we sort of got onto him, but not before he had befriended us," said Basil adding, "I always wondered what you folks were doing in the Syria. Ken told us you were studying ancient biblical places before it became so dangerous to be there."

"Let me explain," said Russell Rollins, "I'm not surprised that you ask, Basil. Our historial interests took us there. Dr. Mark and I both had vacation time so we arranged to go to the Middle East and our wives graciously agreed to go with us."

"What do you and Dr. Mark do, Russ?" Basil asked.

"We are part of a team in Boston involved in the study of dementia. We're working within a Federal research grant. Our intent is help find prevention and hopefully a cure for Alzheimer's disease. Unfortunately it's the same thing our dear friend Kenny is afflicted with. Are you familiar with it?"

"Vaguely. Suzanne and I have talked about it since we heard of Ken's problem. I was just thinking, Suzanne said something that might interest you. Hey, Suzanne come on over here a minute would you please? I want you to tell Russ what you said about repetitious stuff and your hunch."

"Oh, Hi Mr. Rollins. Gosh, Basil, I was just guessing around."

"Please go on young lady and please call me Russ."

"Well, the other day I said to Basil that the incessant repeating of thoughts and our dumbed down sameness of life's activities could possibly be a cause of onset Alzheimer's."

"That is an interesting thought, Suzanne. Go on please," Rollins asked.

"It's only a wag sir, but overuse or unused connectivity just might be the something that causes a neurodegenerative disorder in the brain. They tell me it's gradual and that the most obvious and first noticed fault is declining memory."

Kay called Suzanne, "Suzanne, would you please give us a hand with the table?"

Suzanne excused herself and went to help.

"I want to talk with your wife some more, Basil. Tell me, what were her university studies, and one other question, what is a wag?"

"Her major is psychology, sir. I think she was trying to be funny, a wag is a wild-ass-guess."

Rollin's laughter reached all corners of the house. "I want to talk to you too, Basil. Tell me, what is your speciality, Basil?"

Basil felt a buzz well above his emptied wine glass. Maintaining his composure he whispered, "Mathematics, sir."

Kay announced luncheon. The circling guests found their seats and stood quietly knowing that Kenny by tradition would say grace. Several moments elapsed. Kenny spoke, "Wait! I'll say grace," he offered a profuse thanks for the repast and smiling all around sat down."

⊷ ⊶

"Mark and I are going to take a walk. Good for the digestion you know," Russell Rollins smiled as he and Dr. Bauer headed out the door.

"So, what's this about, Russ?" Bauer asked as they got beyond earshot.

"I think we should get Kenny up to the lab for a few days. Don't you agree that he's only marginally afflicted?"

"Appears to be. Let's see if Kay will let us borrow him for a few days."

"I wish we had known about this earlier. It's been nearly a year since we've seen him."

"Can't help it. We didn't know. Maybe Kay could stay there with Kenny. They could have that small suite on the first floor." Dr. Bauer said.

"I'll ask her when we get back. I'm sure she would like to be with him and it will be good for him."

The men were silent for a while as they walked and finally Dr. Bauer asked, "What are those two, Basil and Suzanne, doing these days?"

"They just got back from Turkey. I think it was yesterday. Did you know they're recent graduates?"

"Didn't know. What about them?"

"The qualifications are in our ballpark. He's a math major. Hers is psychology. I recall they were practicing journalism over there."

"Might be worth a look, Russ. Kay told me that she had to stop their program, the one Kenny had them on."

"We need some specialists pretty soon. This is a good time to hire for the work program. Maybe they would continue at the university. I'll check it out. By the way, Mark, did you notice anything?"

"Nothing other than Suzanne is pregnant."

"Live with that?"

"Oh yeah. Remember though, no drugs! Hey look, you tell them about the lab and if they bite ask for their records. Explain the educational opportunity within the work program, would you?"

"I'll talk to them after I talk with Kay, today."

"Okay. And I'll ask Kay to see if she wants to live at the lab while we see what we an do for Kenny," said Bauer.

⚊⊰⊱⚊

The Porters lived in keyed up anticipation. Every word spoken served to seemed to balance the odds of their entering the world offered by Dr. Bauer and Mr. Rollins.

"Time to drop by the post office again, Basil," urged Suzanne as he loaded groceries in the Jeep. A quick stop at the P.O. on Route 6A, Sandwich, would answer their fated expectation.

"We got mail!" called Basil as he rushed to the Jeep.

"Let me open it," said Suzanne offering her outstretched hand.

She noted the envelope's return address: *Enhanced Neuro Imaging LCC,* "This has to be it, Basil," as she tore the envelope open.

"They did, they did!" Shrieked Suzanne.

"What, they did what?" He demanded.

"They hired us," she replied excitedly sliding out of the Jeep and running to the driver's side, "Get out! This deserves a magnanimous hug!"

Basil complied. The lovers displayed their affection to the delight of the clustering patrons at the post office.

"One more time," Basil declared, "and we really should move along."

Back at the cottage, Basil said, "We're gonna be on a super learning curve at *Neuro Imaging.*"

"You don't think they're doing anything weird up there do you?"

"Nah. When I got talking to Dr. Mark he explained the use of mathematics in determining the biological formation of the Neocortex. I've just begun to realize how much is in front of us."

"Likewise I'm sure," she replied weakly. "I've got one for you smarty, just when did you decide to accept the job?"

"Well, gosh, don't know. I guess it was when they offered it."

"And today, when I opened the letter and told you we were accepted? Somewhere you made a decision. Was it your illusionary free will or was there a little-ole gremlin up there that said 'yes'?"

"I don't know, Suzanne. I surely don't remember actually thinking about accepting, I just knew I would."

"Just think about who's up there running your head."

"Are we headed for a showdown between your psychology and my math?"

"Not at all. I'm only reminding you of our conscious mind or the possible multiples thereof and that thing called the subconscious."

"We've been asked to report for work within a week. Do you think we can locate somewhere near the lab?"

"Somewhere near a hospital too," said Suzanne.

"You mean?"

"Yes, I mean."

Basil sat pensively staring out the window mesmerized by the sight of the incoming tide and the white rivulets returning to the source. His reverie recalled Suzanne as she fed the seagulls on that first morning, then the realization how love gave them life and soon a family.

Suzanne hesitated to disturb her husband. She sensed the presence of a rare moment of bliss. She went to the bedroom and knelt at bedside. Clasping her hands in prayer she felt the babe within kick. Her extreme serenity floated in a loving surround of the Spiritual. Her temptation to search for God through Mysticism lost its allure as she meditated, asking, "What manner of metaphor will my mind conjure to reveal life's meaning?" Suzanne reaped the whirlwind in the cloud of mindful interstices. The Divine manifested and she knew that God's presence was within. Basil felt a shift from his illusory paradise of childhood, and his hobby horse, Topaz. He confirmed what he had always thought: The enduring love of two people who've found God trumped all. He called his beloved, "Once again we're standing together in that sunny faraway forest, Suzanne."

He received her thought, "It's a paradise, Basil."

"I know now what is revealed. No need of the prophets nor the den of the world's philosophers."

"I too. The love of all sentient beings and the mosaic we behold."

They returned to today's consciousness and embraced silently.

Later as they sat at the kitchen table drinking coffee. "I'm so glad we can serve mankind, Basil."

He held her hand, "My dearest Suzanne, we've found our bliss."

www.ingramcontent.com/pod-product-compliance
Lightning Source LLC
Chambersburg PA
CBHW050450290526
45786CB00006B/2235